Virtue & Affluence

The Challenge of Wealth

D1056022

Virtue & Affluence

The Challenge of Wealth

John C. Haughey, S.J.

Sheed & Ward
Kansas City

Sheed & Ward™ is a service of The National Catholic Reporter Publishing Company.

Library of Congress Cataloguing-in-Publication Data
Haughey, John C.
    Virtue and affluence: the challenge of wealth / John C. Haughey.
        p.   cm.
    Papers based on presentations made at weekend workshops in Washington, D.C., 1991.
    Includes bibliographical references.
    ISBN: 1-55612-811-8 (alk. paper)
        1. Wealth—Religious aspects—Christianity. 2. Rich people—Religious life. 3. Wealth—Moral and ethical aspects. 4. Rich people—Conduct of life. 5. Christian ethics. I. Title.
BR115.W4H38 1997
241'.68—dc21   97-2388
                                                                      CIP

Published by: Sheed & Ward
                    115 E. Armour Blvd.
                    P.O. Box 419492
                    Kansas City, MO 64141-6492

To order, call: (800) 333-7373

Cover design by James F. Brisson

www.natcath.com/sheedward

Contents

Introduction

Beginning in 1991, I had the great privilege of conducting a series of weekend workshops for Christian people who had considerable wealth – mostly multimillionaires. They were looking for an opportunity to reflect on their responsibilities or "call" with respect to their wealth. They wanted to do this with those who had a similar kind of "fortune," and to be led by someone who could shed light on their personal reflections and sharings. They believed, in general, that such light would come from the Gospels. What follows is something of a record of my efforts to satisfy their expectations. The groups I led in these workshops strongly encouraged me to give the ideas I communicated a more permanent life than the spoken word. What you have, therefore, in this thin volume are approximations of these presentations.

The nontechnical character of these talks (they are more like meditations than lectures) gives the volume a certain realism. A number of them were interrupted by observations or questions from the participants. These are often included in the text.

The group that gathered the participants and convoked these sessions was the nondenominational Church of the Saviour in Washington, D.C. More specifically, its Ministry of Money "church," with its tireless, zealous leader, Don McClanen, and Dale Stitt, his assistant, had conducted many "money workshops" around the country. Their experience led them to believe that the very wealthy needed a different kind of input and a separate convocation from those who enjoyed lesser means. Don asked me to conduct these weekend workshops, in part because of a book I had published, entitled *The Holy Use of Money*. I am indebted to him for the confidence he placed in me, both for giving me the leadership of the workshops and for encouraging the idea of having the presentations published. I am also very much in the debt of Jim Benda, Don's administrative assistant, who labored indefatigably over the recorded transcripts, trying to make sense out of the often odd way I have of expressing myself or of thinking out loud from notes that are not yet a prepared text.

The groups that gathered annually were both normal and abnormal. Normal in the sense that they felt very much their need for more light on the subject of their financial resources. Abnormal because these resources loomed large in their lives, since they were considerable. It came as a surprise to me how heavy money can get for such folks. I was unprepared for the isolation that considerable wealth creates – the participants seemed really happy to be gathered together to hear and to open themselves to others with like experiences. The groups were from every conceivable denomination of Christianity. Their faith was of great importance to some; others were much less sure of its power. Many participants were blessed with inherited wealth; some others aquired it entrepreneurially. There were as many women as men, as many single or widowed as married. Workshops usually numbered around thirty participants.

The question of my competence to address the groups on this subject was always before me, since I had never had to worry about money, having promised at the ripe old age of nineteen a perpetual vow of poverty – to own nothing. However, my competence or lack thereof didn't seem to bother the participants, since they remained once they came, encouraged others to come the next year, and strongly encouraged the present volume. Whatever competence I bring to the subject I see as having accrued over the years by my use of the Spiritual Exercises of Ignatius Loyola. Since he plumbed the human heart and saw into God's ways in depths I am still attaining, he is the one I am most indebted to for whatever of value the reader finds here.

This volume may have a broader appeal than simply to the wealthy. Not only are members of the middle class intrigued by the wealthy – the American equivalent of royalty – but they are bedeviled by many of the same questions that bother those directly addressed here. Our culture creates in many of us aspirations to the kind of affluence these participants know. Understanding their condition might diminish our appetite for that degree of affluence.

John C. Haughey, S.J.
Feast of St. Ignatius of Loyola, 1996

1

A Sociology of the Very Wealthy

In these sessions we will be reflecting on wealth in the light of faith. To introduce such reflections, I propose a bit of sociology to explain to the wealthy who they are, not in terms of their wealth but in terms of their consistencies with others of their financial condition. While each wealthy person feels as singular as the rest of us, it is interesting how similar they are to one another. Their common characteristics begin to show up when a representative population of wealthy people is interviewed in depth and their responses are compared and analyzed. These constants should be revealing both to the wealthy and to the non-wealthy. The distinctiveness of the wealthy and the problems and opportunities that wealth poses will be seen by an analysis of their autobiographies, from which a sociology of wealth can be developed.

The principal source for this information is Dr. Paul Schervish, a sociologist who is director of the Social Welfare Research Institute at Boston College. He and his research associates have done in-depth interviews with 130 multimillionaires, and have used the autobiographies they supplied to develop a picture of the constants that kept cropping up in their interviews.[1] One-half of the interviewees had inherited their wealth, and the other half had accumulated it through their own entrepreneurial ef-

---

[1] Paul G. Schervish, Platon E. Coutsoukis, and Ethan Lewis, *Gospels of Wealth: How the Rich Portray Their Lives* (Westport, CT: Praeger Publishers, 1994), p. ix.

forts. About two-thirds of them were male. Most had a net worth of around five million dollars, with 44 below that total (though none less than a million) and 27 in excess of ten million. They were randomly chosen for the interviews, some coming from the Forbes 400 list of the very wealthy and others from those with somewhat "anonymous" fortunes.

It turns out that the personal identity of the wealthy is forged much more directly and intimately from their wealth than is the case with the rest of the population. Through wealth the wealthy construct their identities and their worlds. A major part of their socialization into the world is by being taught "the objective rules of money." Their wealth becomes the primary means for developing a will about how they relate to the world, and they express themselves in terms of the purposes their wealth makes possible.

The very wealthy enjoy unique freedoms. First, there is a freedom from the necessity of having to earn their daily bread. Consequently, there is also a freedom to choose among alternative realms of involvement in order to make their marks in the world. With their freedoms they can create a space over which they exercise control, a "fortress of independence, a citadel of command, a visible outpost that secures their dominion in more than one place at the same time."[2]

This special space they are able to stake out is partly territorial. They are able to cordon themselves off from unwanted intrusions by having special residences, valets, security guards, limousines, etc. This special space is also psychological; it develops sequentially in two phases. In the first phase the wealthy develop a worldview that places them at "the controlling center of their social in-

[2] Ibid., p. 4.

volvements." They have identified their interests and see themselves as entitled to pursue them. In the second phase they begin to evaluate the spiritual and moral quality of these interests, seeing them more in terms of public needs they are able to meet rather than seeing them in terms of personal needs or private interests. In this second phase they begin to discover the spiritual secret of money, as Schervish calls it. By this he means that money need not enslave; it can liberate and enable those who have it to establish empathetic bonds with and care for others.[3]

Before wealth is experienced by the wealthy as a blessing that carries responsibilities, it is often experienced as a burden, even a curse, especially by those who have inherited it. Wealth often distances those who inherit it from their peers, making them unsure of themselves and of the motivations others have for relationships with them. It can also be experienced as a source of guilt, especially when there is a dark side (factually or by dint of the absence of information) as to how it was acquired. No less a burden develops when other people make the wealthy a target of envy, jealousy, or dunning. Finally, when there is a fragile sense of self-worth, inherited wealth can lead to a life of low self-esteem, especially when the wealth is accompanied by no sense of personal accomplishment.

While theological and religious literature speak of conversion, anthropology is fond of the term "liminality" to convey a similar process. Limina are thresholds the person goes through, each more mature phase superceding a less mature one. The wealthy have a number of

---

[3] Paul G. Schervish and Andrew Hennan, *A Study on Wealth and Philanthropy, Final Report* (Chestnut Hill, MA: Social Welfare Research Institute, 1988), p. 209.

stages peculiar to them that they must go through to deal
with their opportunities. Failing this, their wealth can easily become an obstacle to growth in personal appropria-
tion and authenticity.

Humans make their mark on the world by agency,
by being moral agents who pursue purposes, make
choices, do deeds. The wealthy who successfully manage
their potentially burdensome situation find themselves
blessed with hyperagency in the sense that they can do all
that the rest of us can do, but they do it in spades. They
can shape their own ways and influence the conditions
and circumstances of their lives in ways the non-wealthy
can scarcely imagine.

With the extra freedom the wealthy enjoy they build
what Schervish aptly calls "principalities." In varying degrees the principalities enable the wealthy to enlarge
their own "realms of command" by influencing circles beyond themselves, such as government and culture. Their
distinctiveness resides in their ability "to align institutions
to their wills rather than simply jockey for advantage"
within the network of institutions that the nonwealthy
have continually to do.[4] The value of the power the
wealthy enjoy is familiar to society. It revitalizes institutions, it supports health programs, funds educational, cultural, and religious initiatives and keeps political parties
hearty. Indeed philanthropy would be obsolete if the
wealthy were not in the habit of making their private resources available to meet unfulfilled needs. In some
cases, they are the supporters of or contributors to private-sector initiatives. But as often as not they are the
creators or entrepreneurs behind public philanthropic
endeavors.

Principalities and the wealth that constructs these

---

[4] Schervish, Coutsoukis, and Lewis, *Gospels of Wealth*, p. 9.

quasi-sovereignties are a moral matter if there ever was one. Schervish has found that in the telling of their stories, the wealthy invariably narrate a dialectic of fortune and virtue. "By means of disciplined effort and strength of character – *virtue* – the wealthy repeatedly attempt to transform the circumstances they face – *fortune* – into something better or more satisfying." They see virtue as necessary for "amending their fate."[5] Virtue, which he calls the habit of doing good, legitimates and enables the wealthy to clothe their lives with a robe of righteous responsibility.

Schervish is a sociologist and as such is interested in making sense out of the world of wealth and the wealthy. What he discovered is an elite who recount their life stories as morality plays. These tales have an outer world that is notable for its empowerments, and an inner world that is notable for the supervision of fate by virtue. In this they are not unlike Andrew Carnegie, who forged a gospel of wealth by linking his very successful accumulation and distribution of wealth with the moral dictates of Providence.

The non-wealthy, who are often emotionally involved with accounts the wealthy give about themselves, cannot help wondering about rationalization and self-deception in those autobiographies. But an a priori resentment or a prejudgment of greed or hardnesss of heart toward the less fortunate are unfair attitudes to take to the life stories of the wealthy or, at least, are no more warranted than a reading of anyone's life story should be. Autobiographies, unless there is good reason to suspect otherwise, must be given the benefit of the doubt that they tell autobiographical truth rather than represent an effort to deceive themselves or the hearer/reader. The in-

---

[5] Ibid., p. 11.

terpreter of the accounts analyzed has observed: "In telling their stories, the rich are more novelists than liars. They may spin lofty tales, but they do so to make meaning rather than to mislead."[6] Unlike the non-wealthy, those who have come into wealth either by inheritance or by entrepreneurial initiative have plenty of inducements to take social responsibility, obligation to society, and civic duty seriously, often from an early age. This message has usually been dinned into them from their earliest experience of wealth.

Sociology has the value of thinning out particularities so that a clearer picture of the phenomena being inquired about can be developed. It has its limitations, too. The particularities experienced by any given person of great wealth can seem to be unaccounted for or bunched into generalities that evacuate their uniqueness. Admitting these limitations but convinced of the value of the overall picture herein contained, we proceed to the next consideration. In what follows there are a number of considerations by which the very wealthy can take the measure of themselves.

For Reflection

To what extent do the wealth autobiographies described in this chapter mirror my way of coming to terms with my own financial resources?

In what ways does the profile developed by the Schervish study deviate from my way of understanding myself and my wealth?

---

[6] Ibid., p. 271.

2

Is Money Faithful?

The autobiographies of the wealthy mentioned earlier indicate how the wealthy develop an understanding of themselves in relation to their wealth. The subjects or authors of those autobiographies would profit from considering Jesus' insight that there is something about wealth that is treacherously fickle. It as insubstantial as a moth-eaten garment that shreds in your hands. I would like to contrast the fickleness of wealth with the constancy and faithfulness of God.

It would be interesting to go back and examine how the conviction about the faithfulness of God grew in Israel. I think you would find that it developed in those who didn't have anything concrete they could rely on, beginning with the Israelites in Egypt, then the sojourners in the desert, the exiles in Babylon, and the 'anawîm in established Israel. These have all left us testimonies of their conviction that God is faithful and can be relied on.

Those who have something tangible to count on do not need God. Those who live affluently and concentrate on things do not even notice God's faithfulness. Faithful Israel had no such affluence and was in critical need of a faithful God. The "faithful" in Israel learned to rely on the fact that God had initiated a covenant with Israel that tied God to Israel, notwithstanding their infidelities. Israel rejoiced in and continuously celebrated this covenanted commitment that unmistakably revealed God as faithful. Even Israel's unfaithfulness did not make God other than faithful, though it dimmed Israel's ability to see this quality in God.

Israel's heart was paradigmatic of every human heart. The best way to learn to rely on God as rock is to not have other rocks to rely on. I presume this is why Jesus warned us to beware of riches, since they seem to be more substantial than they are. Paul Tillich made a comment about intermediate things like wealth that we try to make ultimately substantial when he observed that "idolatry is the elevation of a preliminary concern to ultimacy." Although God's faithfulness is ineradicable, knowing about it is contingent on our needing God to be faithful. If we don't, whether God is faithful is neither here nor there; it is a matter of no practical import. Maybe that is why Jesus described as woes (Luke 6:24-26) having our fill now, having our consolation now, being financially secure now because God's faithfulness can then become irrelevant. We needn't cling to the saving story of God's faithfulness if we have found something that can substitute for the security it has provided our countless forbears and contemporaries. They were "the faithful" because that divine quality stamped itself on their hearts and lives. They came to believe in the Faithful One and began to reproduce the same quality in their lives. I am not implying that those with some degree of economic security are incapable of a covenantal relationship with God, nor that religious commitment requires placing ourselves and our families in financial hardships. What I am saying is that having financial security can lead to a lessening of our religious sensibilities and of our perception of God as the only real security we have.

Before our feet can feel the rock, they feel the insubstantiality of the water. Relying on God's faithfulness takes some doing because "faith is confident assurance concerning what we hope for and conviction about things we do not see" (Hebrews 11:1). Making it from the water to the rock is a gift because what we are looking to stand on isn't visible to the eye of flesh. The first gift is faith; the second gift is to live with so firm a conviction about God's faithfulness that it can make and keep us faithful back, so to speak, notwithstanding long periods of invisibility.

We cannot be faithful to God if we do not first perceive God's faithfulness to us. And we will not see this quality in God if we are relying on something else or if our attention is elsewhere hence never noticing this about God. We won't be faithful to God if we don't see God's faithfulness to us. If we do perceive God's faithfulness then we will live relying on God and our choices will be taken in the light of that conviction.

Ignatius of Loyola has an interesting meditation in his Spiritual Exercises that can concretize these remarks. He imagines three people unexpectedly inheriting a large sum of money and sees them handling the situation in three different ways. There are several constants, however, about these three types. Each believes in God and is more than slightly interested in gaining eternal life. Each also feels uneasy about the newly won inheritance, since its acquisition has not yet been integrated with the spiritual life. The reason for the meditation is Ignatius's perception that the heart easily migrates from a treasured relationship with God to a treasure that is not God. This is an extremely important moment, therefore, in the heart history of the three, given the highly seductive quality of newly won wealth. The rapid growth of the gambling industry and the widespread popularity of state-run lotteries are contemporary evidence of this.

Ignatius instructs those undertaking this particular imaginative exercise to begin by asking God to bestow on them "the grace to choose what is more for the glory of

His Divine Majesty and the salvation of my soul." At the end of reviewing the three different responses and reflecting on their own dispositions about the matter, they are to undertake a petitionary form of prayer first to "Our Lady," whom Ignatius believed had the same power to influence her son as she did at the marriage feast of Cana. Next, they are to petition Jesus to obtain the favor of seeing and choosing what would be for the greater glory of God if there were a particular matter not yet integrated into their lives. Finally, they are to petition God, the giver of all good gifts, to bestow the gift of light and the power to choose what would be for God's greater glory.

The imagined first person (or type of person) feels moved to get rid of the attachment to the windfall inheritance, since it is a source of distraction and unpeace, "but the hour of death comes and they have not made use of any means." The attraction to the attachment and the desire to be rid of its negative consequences neutralize each other, so that no action is taken. God's love and faithfulness do not prove strong enough to bring the person to a decision that would resolve the split in desire.

The second person (or type) is more proactively "devout" about the matter. He enlists God to come around to what he wants, which is to retain the sum he has acquired. He does not "decide to give up the sum of money in order to go to God, though this would be the better way" for him. He, therefore, has created for himself the good fortune of having God and the sum lumped together, of having his cake and eating it too.

The third person (or type) is the most interesting. She puts an affective distance between herself and the inheritance in order to regain her prior integrity as she awaits orders about the disposition of the sum "as God our Lord inspires" her. She has placed it in an escrow account, so to speak. It is over against her now and, therefore, is not so mixed in with her identity that she sees who she is as defined by what she has. Her disposition of "disponibilité" toward God enables her to get on with her life, being a faithful servant of God and a follower of Christ. Meanwhile she awaits anticipated interior movements in order to discern while she notes the changing exterior circumstances in which she finds herself. Both have to be weighed so as to come to a decision about what would be to the greater glory of God with respect to the disposition of the inheritance.

The meditation is not about choices, but takes an inventory of the heart and its dispositions. The heart can find itself divided and by dint of indecision remain so, as we saw with the first person. It can talk itself into having it both ways, as the second person did. Or it can dispose itself to be moved by God while actively becoming free of what was initially seductive, as the third person became. This latter disposition presumes that one has really become free not because of any superiority of will or any excess of virtue but because of a sense of identity in the Lord from whose love and faithfulness one had previously drunk deeply. This would explain the third party!

There are innumerable evidences of God's faithfulness, most of them tangible, for those who see with the eyes of faith. It should be noted, however, that it is easy to go from relying on God to relying on what was initially taken to be tangible evidence of God's faithfulness The prayer of gratitude keeps this disorder from developing. This same kind of prayer can keep us from taking the faithfulness of God for granted.

For Reflection

Luke 12:33-34: "Get purses that do not wear out, treasure that will not fail you, in heaven where no thief can reach it and no moth destroy it. For where your treasure is, there will your heart be also."

3.

"For Me to Live Is . . ."

Fill in the following blank: For me to live is_____. This is a cardinal question – what/who is closest to my heart? What gives me life? It is not a geographical question – Where do I live? A bit of introspection will unearth an extremely important factoid. Is it my family? a particular person? my job? my reputation? drink? golf? truth? guilt? fear? pain? productivity? status? God? security? peace of mind?

How we fill in the blank is a good indication of our spiritual condition. What is being given primacy of place in your heart? Does it deserve it? Should it be dislodged or should it be reaffirmed? It is functioning as your pearl of great price for all practical purposes, even though you might not really esteem it in the clear light of day.

The text that prompts this exercise is Paul's bold assertion: "For me to live is Christ!" (Phillippians 1:21). This is a remarkable statement that Paul is, in effect, so taken by the reality of someone else that he lives for this other, this Christ. Often Paul states that he lives in this other, in Christ. The only explanation for this and the only experience that approximates it is the love that has brought about this union.

Paul's claim prompts several legitimate questions. Is he exaggerating? Judging from the rest of his writings and his life, the answer seems to be no, he's not. Is he a fanatic? Is it psychologically healthy to so totally identify with Christ? It surely would have been unhealthy for Paul if he didn't have a fully formed identity that he freely chose to invest. But he most assuredly did. And he made it wholly available to Christ. Judging from his letters it wasn't an instant surrender. Over time, gradually, what he had counted as gain he began to see as loss as Christ became his wealth, as he put it (Phillippians 3:7-8). Gradually, Christ galvanized his energies and captivated his imagination and came to be Lord of his life. Paul yielded up his personhood in love to Christ and him crucified. Imagine what this says about his interior life – his heart, his mind, his purposes – if he can say, "For me to live is Christ."

In a sense the statement represents Saul's description of his third metamorphosis. The perfect Pharisee was his first and his second one was Paul, the apostle to the Gentiles. Mind you, this is not simply a statement about Paul's beliefs. So it's not as if Paul said, "Since I have been baptized into Christ I believe the life of Christ is in me; I believe that the Spirit of Christ indwells me." He did more than believe these things, which I presume we all believe. He took these beliefs to heart with such abandon that they became an actual experience of his selfhood being lived in and for and through another. So much was this the case that Paul adds a reality check to his contention that for him to live is Christ, namely, "for me to die is gain. . ." It would be the gaining of complete union with the one who has become my life in the flesh (Phillippians 1:21).

God's grace will have triumphed in me when I see my dying as gain, not loss, since through it I will gain what my heart most profoundly seeks, namely, to see Christ face to face. The only thing that can explain this kind of enthusiasm is love, which always seeks union with the beloved.

Another question prompted by Paul's claim is, Does it make one narrow? Did it make Paul a narrow person? Obviously not! His letters teem with passionate expressions of love for particular people and congregations. I think of Gerald Manley Hopkins's line when I think of Paul: "For Christ plays in 10,000 places, lovely in limbs and lovely in eyes not his / To the Father through the features of men's faces."

The better line of questioning is directed not at Paul nor at the text but at ourselves. If the statement represents the pinnacle of living for a Christian, we might ask ourselves why this has not become our experience of Christ, perhaps not even our aspiration in life. One reason is to assume that "for me to live is" wrapped up in self-identity. On reflection it seems obvious that in our own being is never enough; that there is an ongoing acquisition that we seek in order to fill the void that we find in ourselves. The anthropology behind this statement sees human beings having to transcend themselves to find themselves. Or as the Gospel puts it: "Whoever would save his life will lose it, but whoever loses his life for my sake will find it" (Matthew 16:25).

Honestly, unabashedly making the statement, "for me to live is Christ," does not represent the annihilation of my identity, any more than it did for Paul. Rather, it is an incomparable achievement, an achievement that would make any other pale by comparison. What better measure of success in life could be found than this one?

What are the possibilities of this state of union for the rest of us run-of-the-mill types? I have known several prison chaplains who have pastored on death row and a number of hospital chaplains who knew the interior life of those who finally dealt with who they were and what their lives were ultimately meant to become. They would suggest that Paul's statement is not an exaggeration but an accurate description of what some inmates or patients say about their hearts and their spiritual condition. If this is an attainable height, how much of our lives we waste distracted by other things!

Let each one of us examine our own relationship to this Pauline profession of faith, hope, and love. Is it even an aspiration? If it isn't, should it be? If it should be, could it be? We might contend that this degree of union with Christ was peculiar to Paul and is not available to the rest of us. This argument would not go very far, given the nature of Christian baptism. We were all baptized into his death, from which we rose a new creation, each of us radically changed from who we were before the symbolic drowning of the person existing in the old creation, the "old man." Baptism's radical rebirth is evidence of the heights to which the new person is called. Given baptism we could reiterate with Paul that "I indeed have been taken possession of by Christ Jesus" (Phillippians 3:12). Consequently, "I live now, not I but Christ lives in me."

Living in, with, for, and through Christ is not our idea, nor is it a feat we are capable of performing solo. It is not doable simply by willing it. On the other hand "nothing is impossible with God" (Luke 18:27). Is it, therefore, the will of God for you and me that for us to live "is Christ"? It most assuredly is. That was the import of our having been baptized into his death and of every sacrament we have received since that moment.

If this way of viewing baptism and the sacraments and the word of God we read in Church is appropriate in our personal prayer, if these approximate our understanding of the Christian vocation, then we must become what we already are! Become by our wholehearted choice and by our own desires what God has already begun to make us by grace, by God's own action. Namely what?

Christ's own. The intent of God's work in all of us is to yield ourselves wholly over to Jesus in faith, hope, and love.

It would be good to know God's will about your wealth. I don't have any idea what this is. What I do know is that you are to consider anything that is not Christ to be so much rubbish by comparison, so that he might be your wealth (Phillippians 3:8). If he is your wealth, then your wealth and your disposition of your wealth will become a means to the end of deepening your union with Christ. If he is not your wealth, you must ask God to change your heart about his Son and about your fortune, even asking that God give you a loathing for your fortune if it is diffusing your relationship with Christ or is interfering with it in any way. Wealth must be a means for you to express your love of Him who has brought you out of darkness into his marvelous light; it is never an end in itself, retained for itself.

I ask you to figure out how you fill in the blank in your ordinary, day-to-day life. This is a crucially important question. But do not lacerate yourself if the answer is something less than Christ. Begin where you are, and bring where you are to his attention. The changeover will begin when you name the truth of your spiritual condition and then let God get to your heart through Christ. If you let the process begin, with Paul you can say, "I am confident that the One who has begun this good work in you will complete it on the day of the Lord Jesus" (Phillippians 1:6).

For Reflection

Is Paul exaggerating the link a Christian is to have or can have with Christ?

If he is not, do I aspire to this way of living my life?

If he is, is the way I fill in the blank a fruitful way of living my Christian vocation?

4

A Passion for More

Pleonexia is a Greek word that can be understood as "a passion for more . . . an insatiability for more of what I already experience or have. If I just had a little bit more, I would be happy." (I would be financially secure; I would not have this gnawing uncertainty – if I just had a little bit more. . .).

"Avoid pleonexia in all its forms" (Luke 12:15) – this lust for more; this libido for more control, more satisfaction, more knowledge, greater financial security. "Avoid pleonexia in all its forms" – and it takes many forms, even spiritual forms.

In Greek philosophy, virtue is always a mean between two extremes. Pleonexia is an extreme needing to come to a mean. Pleonexia means too much of a good thing. It has to do with excess. God designed us with a desire for more, a desire always reaching for the infinite. Pleonexia is a profound miscalculation about what this more is that we are scripted to desire.

A person may be wealthy, but that person's possessions do not guarantee life, security, or happiness. The deception is this: "If I have more of this or that which I desire, just a little more, then I'll have life as a result of this more that I have."

The craved object of our pleonexia always functions as an idol. The object of our pleonexia subjects us to the power of our insatiable desire. We think that if we have more of what we desire, just a little bit more, then we will

have life as a result of this more that we have. Our pleonexia subjects us to the alien power of the object of our
insatiable desire.

"Pleonexia of any sort is forbidden by the holiness
that is in you" (Ephesians 5:3). Pleonexia is a profound
miscalculation about how to deal with our capacity for
infinity. It's an itch that is never relieved, and when this
itch begins to get legs into our culture, it starts showing
its ugliness: drunkenness, infidelity, child abuse, spousal
abuse, rape, militarism. When a critical mass of the citizenry is incited to pleonexia, you have a sick culture. You
have a culture that is propelled by insatiability.

The major activity incited by pleonexia is accumulation. The man with the grain bins in Luke 12:13-21 is
called "fool" because accumulation of grain is making a
fool of him. Any object of pleonexia makes a fool of the
one pursuing it because that object lulls us into thinking
that more of our life comes from that object; and when
we have more of the same, we begin to misconstrue the
right order that God has written into our hearts and into
the world and into things. The fool's favorite word is
"my" – I will pull down my barns. . . . There is no sin
here except the sin of idolatry. No conscious sin is committed except the sin of narcissism . . . my, me, mine!

What is the purpose of the abundance of grain? It is
the same as the purpose of all material and financial
bounty – that all may share in it! The social consciousness of the fool is nonexistent! And whatever spiritual
consciousness the fool had evaporated when the grain as-
sured him that he had life as a result of it. Others' needs
for what he has an abundance of do not even come into
the picture.

People outside our [North American] culture see so
much more clearly that what is peculiar to our culture is
this pleonexia. We have more. We incite the need for

more. Culturally, we reinforce the need for more to make our supposedly free enterprise system grow! The only thing our free enterprise system knows is the law of growth, and it deems this pleonexic growth normal.

If our economy functioned in the mean rather than in the extreme, then we would be the authors of our economy. We are the authors of our economy if it does our bidding, if we use it to pursue our values. We are not the author of our piece of the economy if it dictates to us or tells us what is valuable or tells us what we ought to have in order to be someone, or persuades us what we ought to want.

A basic perversion takes place when a subject becomes an object. Once we succumb to pleonexia, we become objects among other objects rather than subjects determining our lives, rather than the authors of the microeconomic realities that affect our lives.

We live in the extreme, and we think of it as normalcy. We live in an economy that incites pleonexia – for more of what we think we need and for too little of what we really need.

The economy is not the problem. Like the Sabbath, the economy was made for us. We end up (instead) being made for the economy. We become measured as economic units, and we even begin to measure ourselves in economic terms and to measure other people in economic terms.

The problem is not the economy; it is our hearts! The deal that God made with our first parents and all subsequent humans was this: I will make and you will co-make. And as civilization matured, part of the co-making was the creation of economies. Economies are an agreed-upon complex process whereby needs are met from supplies that are made. Each person in a just economy is to exercise the virtue of contributive justice. That is to say, he or she is to be productive, utilizing the work of God's hands and as a result of utilizing God's goods, thus contributing to the common good, the commonweal. Then the common wealth can be distributed according to the needs of people. That was the plan. That was what an economy was for. It was to be a means of production and distribution, with everyone contributing to it and everyone receiving from it.

The problem is that once labor (we) created capital (it), capital started taking on a life of its own. And then capital, because we ceased being its authors due to pleonexia, started dictating to us, rather than we to it. So now we're like a group of hopeless Hannahs; we have lost the wisdom to figure out what to do with the trade deficit, the welfare system, the budget deficit, basic human needs, etc. None of the things we value can be budgeted. The things we don't value have an enormous piece of the budget. We're like objects (economic objects) being impacted by the economy rather than subjects determining the economy.

And all of this starts in the heart, so we can't lament victimhood. It starts in the heart and it starts with this being driven for the more! "The heart is more devious than any other thing, perverse, too: who can pierce its secrets?" (Jeremiah 17:9).

Consumerism, racism, sexism, militarism – all the isms that we are guilty of seem to be due to the fact that we are not seeing "the great hope to which we are called!" (Ephesians 1:18). They are failures in eschatology, if you will. The true object of our hope is either wrong or too remote or just plain dim. Once again, I have recourse to the Spiritual Exercises of Saint Ignatius Loyola. In particular, I want to bring you into his meditation on the two different strategies that all human beings are being subjected to. One of these is Christ's, which we will examine later. Here I only want to comment on the strategy of "the enemy of our souls," whom Ignatius names Satan. As far as Ignatius understands it, this strategy is never out in the open. And since it is hidden, it is all the more successful. It and its author are always behind the scene, scheming how to seduce people into the trap of pleonexia. Here I am using the Aristotelian term we have been examining in this essay to explain Ignatius.

The first step in the strategy is not to get people not to sin (to overdrink or to whore around or the like), rather, the first step is to get people to desire something, which brings this transcendental hope down to something much more immediate. Then they go for it and more of it, focusing upon this more. And once they get more and more of it, then they are socially confirmed for having it or being associated with it. They end up thinking that who they are is what they have! They see themselves and others in terms of what they have. So, first of all they start with ardor for more of "this"! They then receive confirmation of this disordered identity from their associates. The movement is all in one direction. The final stage is independence.

Independence is attractive because we do not have to own our human vulnerability, our mortality, our dependence on God, our dependence on people. "We will be invulnerable!" Like the man with the bins of grain, we aspire is to invulnerability. "We can control everything." The strategy of Satan is that we each become independent. Then what do we try to become as a country? We try to become invincible. Even worse, we try to control everyone else by becoming the "cops" of the world.

This pleonexia strategy is working well and universally. Even the developing countries around the world are saying, "What we want is to be like the North Americans."

It all starts in one heart. One heart incites another heart, and the inciting is never named in terms of pleon-exia. It's never named except with tired words like "materialism." I don't think we can fight materialism by saying, "Boo, hiss, materialism!" which is what we usually do in the churches. What we have to do is bring ourselves to concretely envision the great hope to which we are called, which is not simply an ultimate hope. Our eschatology has moved us back into some future, inaccessible moment when God will ultimately fulfill us. Big deal! That's not hope; at least that's not Christian hope. Christian hope impacts the heart *now*! The right hope and the right accent on hope is the key to money getting back under our authorship. Of all the lore of the the Gospels and theology, hope is the most underestimated piece, I believe.

The greatest thing the churches could do to complement the things it has already done is to begin to develop much deeper inroads into this matter of our hopes – so that people can "give an account of their hopes" and begin to align their little hopes with the great *hope* to which they're called.

Since God has made us capable of infinity, that infinity has to become more tangible for us to pursue it. In lieu of the intangibility of infinity, we have this propensity to fasten onto something that is not God and make a god of it. We have to become more eschatologically sensitive. This is to say that our hopes have to get more real, have to take onto more reality so that the immediacy of those freshly felt hopes can begin to impact the futile objects of our appetites. We are talking about hopes and appetites incited by an imagination inspired by the Holy Spirit. This is the core of the therapy we need.

Jesus told parables to get us to "forefeel" the Kingdom. As you work through the parables, keep in mind the power of the Spirit to work on our imaginations. In this way the power can begin to concretize our hope, so that the object of our hope is not for that which is faint. Rather, all our hopes are integrated and in right order. Matthew 13:44-46 provides examples of parables that invite the imagination to re-envision one's life and purpose. They tell familiar stories, first of the pearl merchant who found a pearl of incomparable beauty and sold all he had to acquire it. The other story is of the treasure hidden in the field that was discovered by a fellow who covered it back up so he could buy the field. In both cases, a meandering heart is given a clear object of hope. It pursues it unswervingly, making all the resources at hand serve the purpose of pursuing a treasured "object," the reality of God, union with God, life lived with, through, and in God.

Remember, the purpose of worship in your life is to make sure that which is of worth, according to your deepest sense, is assigned primary worth and that which is of lesser worth is relative to the deepest worth.

How is it possible to live these ideals, to be so disciplined? What is impossible for us is possible for God. Let us open ourselves to God's power. It can move us into childhood, into dependence on God!

I'm imagining Jesus saying, "Follow me! Don't follow your culture. Follow me! Don't follow your biases. Follow me! What's in it for you? Not a grand name. Not an important ministry. Not even importance. What's in it for you is Me! And I am enough for you. Get in touch with my invitation to you to follow me; get in touch with the resistance you have to the invitation. If you want the resistance to go away, then ask me. If you want to know the source of the resistance, put your finger on it or ask me if you don't know what it is . . . so you can . . . follow me!

He asks you: "Why would you spend a lifetime obediently adhering to the tenets of the church – but resist following Me, being with Me, learning of Me and My heart? What I want is for you to follow Me so that My joy may be in you and your joy may be complete!"

For Reflection

The Aristotelian concept of pleonexia is seen here as a profound – even tragic – miscalculation about the kind of "more" we need to be happy. It would be helpful to reflect on what kinds of "more" I am pursuing and whether they will satisfy me if I am successful in acquiring them.

5

Stewardly Discipleship

Dietrich Bonhoeffer, a pastor of the Reformed tradition, who was murdered by Hitler, wrote tellingly about discipleship. He distinguished between cheap grace and costly grace.

Cheap grace is grace without discipleship – grace without the cross and without Jesus Christ living and incarnate in our lives. The cheapening has turned the grace of Christ into a doctrine, principle, or system. Costly grace confronts us with the gracious call to follow Jesus. It comes as a word of forgiveness through the cross to the spirit that is broken and contrite – broken of its own agenda. It is costly because it costs the person who hears it his or her own life. And it has cost the Father the life of the Son and the Son His own life. That's why it's costly.

Cheap grace is discipleship's greatest enemy because it is such a shrewd counterfeit. It has successfully separated believing from obeying the call. But only he who is obedient believes, not the other way around. There is no lack of Christians who have heard and assented to the faith – who have heard the Word as idea rather than as address. The Word as address comes from on high. It is targeted at the heart and has to be responded to individually by each person.

Conversion, which is what discipleship calls for, involves three connected parts. It involves a change of mind or a change of attitude (a conversion of the intellect). It involves a change of heart (a change of affection; a choosing to fall into loving). Finally, it involves a change of conduct, behavior, lifestyle. For conversion to be total it has to be intellectual, affective, and moral.

If there is at least the desire to follow Christ, then we must ask for the grace to know Him more intimately, love Him more ardently, and follow Him more closely. Once there is an acquiescence, a saying yes to the call, then we can begin to take on His agenda. "He must increase and I must decrease" (John 3:30).

His agenda has everything to do with *The Holy Use of Money* (the title of a book I wrote). It has to do with your resources and how you use them and what you have in mind in using them – to what ends are you using them?

In effect, he said to Peter when he called him, "You cannot follow Me and carry the nets with you. They don't fit where we're going. You have to leave the nets behind."

And we all have nets. It's in the nets we catch the "more" that we knew before the call. We have to leave the nets behind and pursue a "more" that is of a different nature. We are still pursuing a "more" but of a different quality than the "more" we pursued before.

He says: "You must grow rich in the sight of God. And I intend to endow you with that which makes you grow truly rich."

"I the Master, in calling you to follow Me, am asking you to take over a part of My house. It's My house and I'm asking you to take it over – to manage it – to make sure the property brings the increase it is capable of bringing. I'd like you to manage the house and conduct the affairs of the house according to My nomos (My mind, My order, My norms)."

The responsibility of a disciple is captured in the word *oikonomos,* a noun combining two Greek words: *oikos,* "house" and *nomos,* "order," or "law," or "norm."

From these words together you get an interesting image usually translated "steward." The steward manages the Master's property according to the mind of the Master. What is the steward manager of? Material things are important. But the first range that the steward is to be master of are the mysteries of God.

You are stewards of the mysteries of God! (1 Corinthians 4:1).

The mysteries of God can be found in all the incidents, scenes, stories, and parables that we find in the Scriptures. The mysteries of God start with creation, and they end with the promise of the new heavens and the new earth. Between these two bookends, every other incident is a "mystery" because it's beyond our human capacity to conjure it up. All we can do is take it in, since it is incommensurate with our minds. All we can do is receive it. And we receive it by contemplation, meditation, and celebration. So the whole liturgical year is a series of mysteries that we take in, give room to, let our hearts be stirred by. And from that celebration, that contemplation, that meditation these then become light for our lives. All the mysteries of Christ – incarnation, resurrection, baptism, epiphany, the multiplication of the loaves, the walking on the water, etc. – are to be taken in and savored.

In effect, Christ says: "The first order of business I am giving you in your following Me is to take into the house of your heart the mysteries of the kingdom of God. . . . What I'm asking you to do as the first responsibility of stewardship is to house those mysteries in your heart so that My mind, My order, My norms, and My way of operating become your mode of operating, my way of thinking, your way of thinking. This conversion is a neverending process, and I am asking you to take more and more time and give more and more space in the room that you have in your heart to house these mysteries. To you has been given the secrets of the Kingdom of Heaven (Matthew 13:11-12). I've conferred those secrets on you. To others I have not given those secrets. To those who have been given, that is you, more will be given. I intend to increase the light that comes from each of these mysteries – the mystery of My passion and My death and resurrection, which you celebrate every year; the mystery of My birth; the mystery of My baptism, the mysteries that span the time of My public ministry. To those that have been given these secrets, more will be given, and they will have them in abundance. But to those who have nothing to show for what I have given to them, even the little they have will be taken away."

There is something more foundational here than the usual way stewardship is conceived. That more foundational level gives light to our path. Without those mysteries received and given room – heart room, mind room – stewardship is always going to be an exercise in economic or financial calculation. Stewards of the mysteries of God – when we give them room and let them in, we learn from them the art of companionship. We learn to live our lives through Him and with Him and in Him! And if the heart that gives them room is lighted by them, then the stewardly disciple becomes like a lamp for others to see the way that leads to life.

Then evangelization is not the statements we make to others. If you house the mysteries to the point that they become light for your life, then you evangelize automatically. That presumes we take personal prayer seriously, and that we take communal prayer seriously. It presumes we participate in the process of celebration step by step as our churches give us the rituals they provide for us. Otherwise stewardship, however it's done and by whomsoever, is always going to be a ministry in which calculation is more important than contemplation. Trying to figure out stewardship will drive you and everybody else bonkers.

It's very hard to communicate to other people what their specific stewardship ought to be in the sense of what their particular monetary outlay ought to be. Therefore, it's critical that it be built on a contemplative basis. Otherwise it will get arid and burdensome and begin to take on the calculus of Phariseeism.

Stewardship must be rooted in discipleship, and contemplation is key to both! If the light comes from Christ and from the celebration of His person and His mysteries, then what will we know about the financial and material resources that are the second level of resources we're given to steward?

In the parable of the wicked husbandmen from chapter 12 of Mark's Gospel, we have a picture of people who forgot what the deal was. They chose to pursue their productivity with such competitive zeal and got so immersed in the "more" they could produce that they "changed their names." They became the owners instead of the tenant farmers. They renamed themselves as owners. They forgot that the oikos was not theirs and they forgot – if, indeed, they ever knew – the nomos according to which they were to manage the oikos.

Who are the messengers in the parable? Who were the people who came from outside the system that was being labored in with such intensity, amnesia, and myopia? They say, "Hey, the owner wants His share of the grapes." They're the people who are marginal to the system, sent by the Owner to remind us whose vineyard it is. In the mind of the Owner, the Owner's share of the grapes is supposed to go to these people who are marginal to the vineyard. The poor enrich us, ironically. The poor are the messengers sent by the Owner to remind us for whom this vineyard is being worked: It is for *all!*

We are becoming increasingly adroit in our capacity to basically ignore the messenger. For example, I recall an article from the *New York Times* from January 1991, in which Robert Reich, then the Secretary of Labor, pointed out, "The successful are in enclaves insisting on being community. And from these communities, which are largely inured against major tragedy, philanthropy comes forth. And the philanthropy, while it once had looked at the alleviation of social problems, is now going more and more to things like the arts and the private universities. What is happening is that a yawning chasm is developing in our country, largely reinforced by the ideology of community in the churches."

Even those who have styled themselves as the most sensitive to the poor are suffering from what is called compassion fatigue. The identity of the last messenger, the Son, is really critical here (Mark 12:7). When does the Son come as messenger? It seems to me, if Matthew 25:31 means anything, that whenever the poor arrive, it is the Son, looking for the Owner's share of the grapes so that there will be a commonweal.

What is the role of "assigning worth" (which is my way of understanding worship)? I see this parable as having a Eucharistic overtone. There is to be regular conferral to God of that which our hands have made – the bread we've baked and the wine we've fermented – as a reminder of where "the other 90 percent" comes from.

In this parable we have, it seems to me, a very suggestive scheme of all that stewardship of material goods is meant to represent. Because of our productivity, we make a living; we might even make a very good living. Our productivity is our way of responding affirmatively to the primary vocation that our first parents were given (Genesis

1:26): "Take dominion over the work of My hands – the birds of the air, the fish of the sea, the vineyards on the land. Take dominion. Bring what My hands have made into the full increase." There are many parables in the New Testament where the Master is adamant about the increase. (The parable about the silver pieces: What did you do with My money? . . . I hid it!) There is an accounting of the resources and the increase that they're capable of producing (Luke 19:11ff.).

What to do with your money is a very difficult question. You get a lot of advice about it, you can do a lot of thinking about it, you also can get into a lot of confusion about it.

In that whole matter of money, every call is unique – absolutely unique – because everybody has a different consciousness, a different series of resources, and a whole bunch of other things unique to them. Other than insisting that what you do with your resources is the way you praise God or the way you occlude your eye from God, I think it is very difficult to give good advice. And that's why I think the advice giving has to be rooted in contemplation of the mysteries of God. I believe those mysteries are light bearing – a lot more light bearing than our various ethical reflections, ascetical reflections, and spiritual reflections on the holy use of money.

So, the order I am recommending is to take responsibility for the mysteries of God; and from responsibility there, go on to discern what you are being called to in this matter of the stewardship of resources such as money, goods, time, talent, and treasure.

If stewardship doesn't come from discipleship, then stewardship turns into a batch of "oughts." And if it's a batch of oughts, we're still playing around with our own or other peoples' superegos. The Church too easily becomes just another source of new guilt.

This is an essential part of the call of Christ – that all the goods of the called be used according to the mind of the One who is calling them. The only norm for the use of goods is continually clarified as we come to know the mind and heart of Christ. He can teach us for what purpose we have the goods we have and to what end we might use the goods.

Some of you don't do well using your imaginations, so parables don't click for you. You are better with principles or norms. What might be of help, to you few, therefore, is the statement of the principle about stewardship that comes, once again out of the sixteenth century, from the one who taught me how to understand the Gospel, Ignatius of Loyola. He articulated the matter we have dealt with in this reflection in a logical, principled way. You might want to examine this "principle and foundation" that begins the Spiritual Exercises.

> Human beings were created to praise, reverence, and serve God our Lord and by this means to save their souls. Everything else on the face of the earth is created for them to help them in attaining the end for which they were created (praise, reverence, and service of God). Hence they are to make use of these things in so far as they help them in the attainment of their end. And they must rid themselves of them in so far as they prove a hindrance to them. Therefore, it is incumbent upon us to make ourselves indifferent to the things that we have or could have – our desire and choice being (that which) is more conducive to the end for which we were created.

For Reflection

There is an end for which you have been made.

There's a way to know and to attain that end.

Let the mysteries of God into your mind and heart so the way and the end can become clear.

Stewardship without discipleship becomes love.

Discipleship without stewardship turns the walk into talk.

6

There Is Giving and There Is Giving

You should know about the different kinds of giving. I will start with tithing, then go into almsgiving, and then get into justice giving.

To understand tithing we need to go back to the beginning of Israel. Take the practice of tithing seriously because it was from this that stewardship developed.

When Israel was still a nomadic people, i.e. when herds provided people's sustenance, a "tenth" of the herd's offspring given to Yahweh began to be Israel's way of saying that "the earth is the Lord's and the fullness thereof." In other words, the portion of the whole inheritance that God has given is made to bespeak the belief that all they had come from God. They wanted to ritualize that; they wanted to make that a clear statement. The tithe was the way in which that was done.

When Israel became more of an agricultural people, there came the first fruits of the produce and a tenth of the grain and a tenth of the oil and eventually a tenth of the tender used in transactions.

As Israel settled down, and a system of religious worship became central to Israel, the tithe exacted became a cultic tax.

These were God's ways of forming the self-understanding of Israelites as stewards.

The steward ran the household of the Lord. With the master absent, the steward was put in charge of the household. The mind of the Master, was learned through the Torah and, in turn, through the yearly celebrations of each of the interventions of Yahweh on behalf of the people of God.

Every communal celebration or liturgical feast convened or reinforced the steward's angle of vision on the mind of the Master regarding how to manage the household of the Master. So tithing was the bottom-line way of manifesting the fact that I believe I am a steward of Yahweh and this is Yahweh's house.

Tithing became, like so many other beautifully begun things in Israel, something fixed by law. By the time Jesus came on the scene, tithing was wretchedly quantified. It had become a neurotic kind of practice. After beginning in the spirit of professing the fact that the earth is the Lord's and the fullness thereof, tithing had fallen into a legalistic, narrow minded, law-fixated kind of mentality.

Recall the two men who went up to the temple to pray, for example. The one proclaimed his self-justification by exclaiming what seemed to himself an act of prayer that he tithed a tenth of all he had among other righteous deeds. The other fellow went up and beat his breast, held his head down and said, "Lord be merciful to me a sinner" (Luke 18:13). He went back home justified while the tither went back with whatever merits he thought he won by comparing himself favorably to the publican.

The motivation behind tithing was simple, namely, the acknowledgment of God's sovereignty; acknowledgment of who is the Master of the household. The result was also obedience. The motivation was identification with Israel, identification with the temple, identification with the synagogue. If it hadn't been for tithing, you would not have had the degree of institutionalization that developed.

Jesus came along, however, and showed an ambivalence about tithing, maybe because He had an ambivalence about the consequences of the institutionalization of religion in Israel. What He did was is to reinforce almsgiving.

Almsgiving was meant to be a spontaneous act of compassion done in imitation of Yahweh's compassion for the needy. So you imitate the compassion of God by spontaneously giving to the poor. Jesus suggests doing it in relative secrecy. Don't go around pounding your chest about it. It began to be connected to a doctrine of redemptive almsgiving beginning in the Old Testament and continuing through the patristic age. For example, in Luke 11:41, "Give alms and everything will be wiped clean for you." It is very interesting that Jesus *reinforces* almsgiving, although He does not dismiss tithing.

Does this say something about His problem with the institutionalized religion of Israel? If so, it also says something to the subsequent centuries of the Church. We go two centuries beyond Jesus and find several Church Fathers claiming that three things totally remit sin: baptism, martyrdom, and almsgiving. So the spontaneous giving of what you have to those who present themselves to you in need out of a motivation of imitating the compassion of God is what almsgiving is all about.

However, neither almsgiving nor tithing became a major part of Christian catechesis because both of them smack of a works righteousness. I cannot make myself righteous by my works. So these acts receive a reduced kind of recommendation on the part of the Christian teaching community.

Two other problems relative to both almsgiving and to tithing need to be mentioned here. First of all, they tend to quantify one's faith in relation to God and neighbor. If you quantify faith in relation to neighbor you can start to get into comparisons and self-righteousness. But a deeper problem with both almsgiving and tithing was the fact that both of them gave a portion. But Jesus taught the *total* gift of the self in following Him and the *total* availability of *all* of one's resources to be disposed of as He called His followers now to this, now to that, now to some other responsibility.

So the pluses on tithing and almsgiving were they reflected the belief that the fullness of the earth is the Lord's and imitated God's compassion. The minuses were how they can tend toward a calculus, a quantifying mentality about faith while the call of Jesus was to "leave everything" and follow Him!

The third form of giving has to do with the giving that is motivated by *justice*. Let me make a couple of comments about giving that is motivated by justice.

The meaning of justice is contained in the Latin phrase *suumcuique tradere,* "to each according to what is their due." For the ancients, justice means giving to each one according to his or her due.

As Christianity comes on the scene we get a different sense about the sacredness of the human person. So what is due to one, given the sacredness of the human person, as Christianity sees it, is different than what the ancients or the pagans or other faiths thought was appropriate to give to each person. So presumably, what is understood as due to a person is further refined (in the person alive to God's revelation).

From Judaism, we take each person as made in the image and likeness of God. There is a sacredness in each person because each is a unique reflection of God, created by God and endowed with immortality. There is an eternity of dignity in each person, in light of being made in the image and likeness of God!

Christianity asks, What is due a person in light of each having been redeemed by Christ? In effect Christ said by His death, "Each person is worth My life." If each person is worth His life, then each person must have infinite worth in God's eyes. And if each person has infinite worth in God's eyes, this should call something forth from us by way of calculation about what we are to do with the resources we have control over in relation to those in need.

A further consideration (also unique to Christianity) about what is due to each person relates to the fact that when I was in sin, God saved me – and not because of anything that was due me. Quite the opposite! In other words, I live a life blessed by God because God has saved me from my sins again and again due to no merit on my part. So the overwhelming motivation for justice action – making sure that human beings have that which is due them given their dignity – has to do with the fact of God's having "justiced" me.

The action God took in and through Christ to save us was to make us right before God. The Greek word for this saving action is *dikaiosune,* meaning "righteousness" – being made right with God. I have been made right with God by reason of my baptism. I have been made right with God subsequently by each act of repentance, which God's own grace has prompted in me. Being right with God has created a situation in which I have the justice of God in me. God has justified me. And with repentance, God continues the process of "justicing" me. God's justicing me is not due me. But because God has justiced me, I am empowered to be in right relationship with God, with self, and with neighbor.

Because God has put me in right relationship with God the Father, Son, and Spirit through no merits of my own and has continued to place me in right relationship with God through no merits of my own, this creates in me a power to be in right relationship with self and with neighbor. The font or source of Christian justice action is this "being made right with God," this being justified by God. What God has done through no merits of my own calls me to live in the world in a particular way. In what way? To live in the world in a way so that I become extremely sensitive to the human dignity of every single human being.

Therefore, a person's unmet and "unmeetable" (i.e. they themselves cannot supply them) needs must make a claim over me. That's the core point! Another person's unmet and unmeetable needs make a claim on me and my resources to respond – whether the person says anything or says nothing. Their humanity's inability to achieve human dignity makes a claim on my action and on my resources. This claim starts in the inner circle of those for whom I already have responsibility but extends beyond that inner circle. Why? Because of what is due each person by reason of his or her humanity.

7

Justice Giving

We have now examined stewardship as well as almsgiving and tithing. Here I would like to create the category of justice giving to round out this theme. As people of wealth and as Christian people, you are inevitably philanthropic. Philanthropy grows out of your sense of "fellow feeling," or a sympathetic disposition toward others' needs. But your philanthropy will be wiser if it complements your natural (or supernatural) charity with a sense of justice. Charity in the emotive sense is voluntary and, therefore, contingent on the good feeling toward the benefitted continuing. But if I am the object of someone's charity I am less sure of on-going help than if I am being dealt with in terms of justice, of what is in some sense due me by reason of my humanity. Here we will review a few basic things about justice.

As you probably know, justice is ordinarily distinguished in a number of ways. Here let's say there is distributive, commutative, and contributive justice. Distributive justice is concerned with distribution, with the just distribution of the material goods of the earth. There are more than three billion people on planet earth with incomes of less than two dollars a day, so we can appreciate the urgent need for this kind of justice. Even in the United States, the ratio between the top 20 percent of incomes and the bottom 20 percent is increasingly disparate; presently it is 9 to 1. You could look at your philanthropy in redistributionist terms.

Commutative justice is contractual, meaning that you are just in adhering to the terms of the contracts you enter into. This kind of justice doesn't appear to have much to do with philanthropy. But contributive justice does. It has to do with each person in a society contributing to the upbuilding of the commonweal for the sake of the common good. Those who cannot contribute, e.g., because of age, disability, lack of skills, etc., insofar as it is possible, should be brought to the point where they can add to the commonweal. Philanthropy can have a lot to do with bringing a citizen to the point where he or she can contribute to society, since this usually presumes there is a functioning structure that is enabling the non-contributor to become a source of contributive justice.

These things then start getting played out, as you know, into more complex formulae. They get played out into the doctrine of rights. Human rights are always the just claims that human beings make on a society by reason of their unmet and unmeetable needs. The doctrine of political rights is something we're comfortable about in our country. In fact we're sometimes progenitors of the doctrine of political rights – that human beings by reason of their humanity must have a chance at self-determination, at choosing their own political leadership, assembly, religious freedom, etc.

The part about human rights that we're *not* comfortable with (they're not written into our constitution and we're still arguing about them), has to do with that aspect of human dignity that relates to the *material* well-being of human beings. We're talking here, if you will, of socioeconomic needs, socioeconomic rights.

Without getting lost in the debate about socioeconomic rights, let me stress the main point, the key point: human beings must have the wherewithal to achieve human dignity materially and politically. If they don't, and if I have resources that would enable them to come closer to realizing their human dignity, I must discern what my particular obligation is with regard to their needs.

Bear in mind that we don't want to be in a situation where in meeting peoples' needs we create in them some kind of diminution of their own humanity, e.g. creating in them a dependency relationship toward those who meet those needs. Dependency *is* a complicating issue in all this.

For the sake of the point being made here, let us assume that the potential benefactor realizes that someone cannot meet his own needs and that the benefactor would not be creating a relationship of dependency by assisting in meeting those needs.

Liberation theology has been helpful in getting many to think about the poor. But it is important to remember that the poor in North America and the poor in Latin America are two different kinds of poor. Therefore, you need a different perspective for how to deal with the unmet needs of the North American poor and with the unmet needs of the Latin American poor. The Latin American poor are poor in part because of the *absence* of structures and therefore of opportunities as well as the deep class division between the haves and the have nots.

It's not so simple in our North American scene. It's not that we are without policies and structures, although we frequently have inadequate welfare policies and clumsy structures. And we don't have as profound a divide between the rich and poor as the one in Latin America.

Therefore, you cannot simply import the option for the poor from liberation theology into the North American scene without putting a "trip" on North Americans. You have to translate it into the more complex social processes we have here and the more complex institutions we have in place to meet those needs.

So what to say about all this? I want to say that we can be pin-headed by thinking only in terms of formulaic tithing and programatic almsgiving, that is to say, in terms of *charity* giving. And we can neglect the more major issues as Jesus puts it in Luke 11:41-42. We can, by concentrating on the little acts, neglect the major acts that have to do with "justice and the love of God."

As the whole world becomes a "global village" we get more and more aware of the enormous disparity in the allocation of resources in our world – in the city of Washington, D.C., in the country of Iraq, in the country of India, wherever. We become daily more and more aware of unmet and unmeetable human needs. Where does that leave us? I just want to give some principles to start the ball rolling.

There are two principles here: (1) what is due a human being is the wherewithal to achieve human dignity materially, socially, personally; and (2) unmet and unmeetable human needs make a claim on the rest of humankind, which is the core issue of justice.

What claim is made on the rest of us when either the freedom to choose the social conditions of life or the ability to choose the material conditions necessary to be self-determining, are lacking to someone? This question has created the rationale for human rights, a rationale located in what is called the natural law. But it is also located in the Christian revelation.

In June 1993, I went to a conference sponsored by the United Nations in Vienna. It was the first conference to examine the rationale for human rights in 25 years. You probably know that we have no alternative internationally than the whole matrix of understandings about human rights. We have no other resource except this concept of what is due a human being. What moral claims can a human being make on the rest of us? That's the only avenue we have to adjudicate conflicts and wars.

The hope was that this conference would eventually help to create sanctions across the world so that where those rights are not met, "bite" (international law) and the moral force of the human community's rejection of those ways of going about doing things would stop governments from inflicting cruelties on their citizens and begin to develop a regime of human rights that citizens and governments alike would observe. (See the appendix, "Vienna Diary").

If we cannot agree more clearly about what constitutes human rights and the sanctions necessary to create that moral environment, we're going to go through decades of everybody killing everybody, endlessly. If there is going to be any global peace in the future, it will be because the dignity of the human person is respected and because what that dignity consists in is agreed upon internationally.

The Christian names human dignity in specific terms and names the motivation for responding to that dignity in terms of what Christ has done for me, what Christ has done for us. That's the motivation a Christian takes to the observance of human rights.

While reflecting on justice giving, you should know there are two kinds of social analysis you can make. The one is called *functional* social analysis. It is familiar to most North American sociologists. You do an analysis of a system or a situation and as a result of the judgments made, and action is taken to get it to move from whatever dysfunctionality it is in back to functionality. The other kind of social analysis begins with the idea that there has *never* been a functioning society here. This society has *always* been dysfunctional. This type of social

analysis which finds that the society has always been dysfunctional, is called *dialectical* – that is, we have to create
an awful lot of havoc in order to bring this thing to a
place of functionality. In the case of Latin American society it would mean to bring the haves and the have nots
into a closer middle-class situation.

Dialectical analysis is what those six Jesuit martyrs at
the University of Central America, San Salvador did.
They could have decided that the university existed to do
what every other university does in this world – get people degrees, get people informed, have "stuff" go in
through the head. They could have chosen that. But instead they decided to have a different purpose from every
other university in the world. They wanted "stuff" coming
up through your feet and in through your hands because
you've experienced the plight of the desperate people as
they would seek to radically change their society. That
choice basically won the Jesuits martyrdom. And it all depends upon what social analysis you do – functional or
dialectical.

If you think our North American society has *never*
been just, then you'll do a dialectical social analysis on it.
If you do a dialectical social analysis on it as a Christian,
you'll end up with probably not martyrdom but you'll
certainly end up working for the marginalized. I don't
think you would end up simply giving all your money
away. I think you would end up giving your money
shrewdly to ensure that different structures came into being.

Justice in the North American situation doesn't have
to do with giving money away. It has to do with creating
opportunities and structures that create a greater possibility for people to come to human dignity. Divestiture
without a particular purpose is a nice clean break between you and your "boodle." But when you get into this

justice analysis, whether you do it functionally or dialectically, you start thinking about what structures and opportunities your resources could help create so that human dignity would be enjoyed by many.

All justice comes down to *action*. But action on behalf of justice, which is looking structurally at how society is functioning, is different than the legal justice where I have a claim against you or you against me and we simply adjudicate the claim and end up with that justice.

Participant: I want to go back to this theme of justice giving. You commented that divestiture could at times be too convenient a way to dispose of one's boodle. I want to share our experience of going through divestiture of our wealth as being a tremendous experience of justice giving that turned out to be an empowerment for us. We came to see that we had a certain quantity of potential empowerment that could be utilized.

It became a question of control for us, whether we chose to control the money or divest ourselves of it totally and put it into the hands of folks who'd be able to utilize it for social change. So in going through this divestiture process, we facilitated a tremendous empowerment for people who had talent and vision but who lacked capital. They were able to do things that we never would have been able to do by keeping control ourselves. It was a really exciting process and we felt empowered ourselves too as we went through it. So I'd like to hold this out as another possibility in relation to justice giving.

John Haughey: Let me unpack what I meant by what might have seemed to be a dismissal of divestiture in relation to justice. What I was thinking about was people who for whatever reason, either a lack of sophistication or from guilt or impatience or a sense of need to be clean or whatever the motivation – simply remove themselves from their inheritance or they give their inheritance away. Your form of divestment was good because you thought through with other people how others could be empowered by the power that was latent in your wealth. Wealth is congealed energy.

You ended up with what you called divestment or divestiture. You lost what you had but empowered many, including yourselves, by what you did. Justice giving may well have as its bottom line divestment, but the best justice giving is that which thinks structurally about how empowerment of the benefited happens.

It is just beautiful to me that the impetus for your divestiture came from your identification with people. The function of wealth is solidarity. And what you're describing was that you had the experience of solidarity, then wealth came to you, and you reduced the wealth in order to retain the solidarity.

Justice giving makes likely creation of solidarity. Almsgiving may be no less loving, but it is unilateral. And it doesn't necessarily imply solidarity. That's why justice giving is such a critical issue. I wouldn't want to say one is better and one is worse. But it's extremely important for us to think in structural terms – when we do, the consequences are solidarity.

Participant: Unless we follow Christ first, we will not challenge our family tradition and history when it comes to our inheritance. Any of us challenging our family history with the disposition of our inheritance know the risk and the cost. But I think that's how demanding Christ is: "Unless you hate your father, mother, brother, sister, or wife you cannot follow me" (Luke 14:26).

John Haughey: My first comment is *Amen!* My second comment is that it seems to me that a lot of the ideals that we have been exhorted to live by, which are valid ideals and come from the Gospel, if they don't have self-acceptance as a base, end up debasing the people who are trying to live them because they circumvent this first act of accepting oneself as loved. So the person who cannot accept herself as loved could expend the whole psychic and spiritual energy of her life trying to be better than she is because she can't stand who she is. We all know people who exhaust themselves at the level of superego. In other words, this is the way I ought to be and until I can perform at the level of the ought then there is self-disparagement – all very subtle.

There is a profound perversion when Christianity is one long experience of falling short of the mark of perfection without ever loving yourself. So it's only a person who can be self-accepting, it seems to me, who can afford to surrender self-determination and be healthy.

For Reflection

In my giving, how much does justice, doing justice, enabling justice to be done, come into play?

"If you give what you have as alms, all will be wiped clean for you. . . . you pay tithes on mint and rye and all the garden plants while neglecting justice and the love of God" (Luke 11:41-42).

8

Singleness of Heart

The purpose that we are pursuing in this inquiry into
wealth and its disposition according to the mind of Christ
is impossible for us to achieve, so we center ourselves on
the One who can do it in us. And we ask that this happen
in us in the gentle way in which You always do that, Lord.

From your initial sharings, I hear a desire in all of
you, a desire to have a singleness of heart. That is the
common note that I hear expressed tonight in very different ways: "to sit loose to money" – "that the role of my
financial situation in my growth process might become
clear" – "to learn what wholeness is around money" – "to
find that the Lord is a money partner with me" – "God is
changing my heart about this subject of money" – "I need
to have a sense of community with brothers and sisters
whereby, through sharing our stories with one another, I
can get my footing more firmly in what this commodity is
in my relationship to God" – "I find myself very awkward
about money" – "I find myself unfree about money" – "I
find myself scared about money." All these statements
coming out of you.

All of you are also somewhat aware of the truth that
"to those to whom much is given, much will be expected." So I'd observe that, although the "formulas" for
each of you are different, you have some sense that much
more is expected of you than you have so far achieved.
And you want money to be a way of showing God your

love. You want money to be a means for expressing your deepest values, what you cherish.

A *singleness of heart* would mean that there is a perfect continuum between our interiority and our activity, especially in our money activity, so that what we cherish, value, and believe in, we do! The tension is thereby reduced and money is made firmly into a means for expressing what we really cherish. That is what I heard from you, and I think therefore that this should be the theme for the weekend, that my heart becomes single.

One of the images from the Gospel that suggests single-mindedness relates to purses. It laments that we feel more secure having two bank accounts or two purses. In the "God purse" we put religious actions, and in the "money purse" we put our money. That way we have two things going for us. We trust in God and trust in a nest egg. We can work it both ways! So when we have to trust in God for whatever reason, we trust in God, and when we have to trust in our nest egg, we trust in our nest egg. Then we don't have to be single-minded or single-hearted. In that way, God becomes one of our possessions. In that way, we don't really have to believe into God, which is what the Greek preposition means when used in that context.

Losing Our Footing into God

We don't believe into God when one foot is "planted firmly on the shore." We believe God but there is no "into" because we haven't lost our footing. The act of believing in God is an act of "losing our footing" into God. Having a double object of trust makes for weak faith. It makes for a "both/and" faith so that I am both a believer and I am also other than a believer. That way I can have the best of both worlds. Faith then is a wager, but it's not a way of life. I always keep a little in the God purse, but it doesn't cost me my life because I always have something in the other purse.

Mammon is money that has become an object of trust. Money is a neutral thing. But money, when it becomes an object of trust, moves out of neutrality (moral neutrality; theological neutrality) and becomes a counterfeit deity. That's what Jesus' complaint was. His problem was with the both/and Israelite mind – where God was an object of trust and God was not an object of trust – the both/and mind can't really trust God enough to let God be God for me or us. One suggestion I'd make is that you not think about money but that you think about the fact that the greatest wealth that you have, that I have, that anyone can have, is God.

What Separates Us from the Love of God?

I think we would all agree that the measure of failure in the life of the Christian, what makes a Christian life a travesty, is to be affectively and experientially separated from the love of God. Conversely, the measure of life's real success is to be inseparably linked to God's love, both affectively and experientially.

If I'm affectively and experientially bonded to God's love, I will respond with love for this God of ours. In that connection, there is Paul's boast in Romans 8:34ff., "Who shall separate us from the love of Christ? Shall tribulation, distress, persecution, famine, nakedness, peril, or the sword? Will any of these separate us from the love of Christ? I am sure that neither death, nor life, nor angels, nor principalities, nor things present, nor things to come, nor powers, nor height, nor depth, nor anything in all creation will be able to separate us from the love of God in Christ Jesus our Lord."

Paul is referring to things "out there"; they cannot separate us from God's love. But there is something that can separate us from that love. That's where the question of wealth comes in. What is wealth doing in my life in terms of being bonded to God's love or being separated from God's love? How is wealth functioning in my life in relationship to this only true measure of success? Is it neutral? Is it functioning neutrally? Is it functioning as a means of growing in union with and love of God? Is my wealth mediating God to me so that my use of it is an "accompanied" use? Christ desires to accompany me in my use of wealth. If that is not the case, aspire to that, so that wealth has a transparency through which I see the will of God and the desires of Christ. And in the use of that wealth, I grow in union with the only "honest-to-God" source of wealth in my life, which is God.

Does my wealth have a window built into it? Does it have a transparency to it? Or is it a dark power that is distancing me from the only real wealth in my life? "Nothing can separate me from the love of God." Those things "out there" can't. Things in the future can't. Nothing can except something that functions as a counterfeit god, as an alternate source of trust. That can separate me, or if not separate me, leave God on hold until I get through the financial activity, the use of resources. Romans 8:34 to the end of the chapter, would be well worth looking at here.

How Does Money Function in My Life?

How does money function in my life? Is it functioning in a way that deepens my union with God? Or is it functioning in a way that postpones my union with God? Is it

functioning in a way that seems to make that union su-
perfluous?

Notice the oneness portrayed in Ephesians 4:4-6:
"There is one body. And in this one body there is one
Spirit. And all of us were called to one hope. And in order to arrive at that one hope, we were given one Lord,
one faith, one baptism to bring us to the one God who is
above all and in all and through all." One hope! The one
hope is that God might be my wealth! Paul speaks also of
this in Philippians 3, that Christ might be my wealth.

I've got to develop an integrity in my heart, and the
only way I can do so is if all that is diffuse now becomes
one. From oneness comes power: the power of faith, the
power of hope, the power of love. People become powerful when they have integrity in the Lord.

Another text you might find helpful is the "pearl"
text, Matthew 13:45-46. "Again, the kingdom of heaven is
like a merchant in search of fine pearls who on finding
one pearl of great value, goes off and sells all that he has
and buys it."

If you haven't found the pearl, and if you're looking
for it, what do you think it will be? What is that pearl for
me? Have I found that pearl? Do I want to find that
pearl? Do I want to have something of such incomparable beauty impact my heart that everything else in my life
fails in comparison, and in fact I am willing to forfeit having it to buy the pearl?

This is the oneness that Jesus is talking about, this
oneness of heart. What I hear in the group is double-
mindedness and a strong desire to be single-minded.

The Addiction of the Heart

In Luke 12:22, Jesus tells us, "Don't be anxious about to-morrow, about whether you're going to have something to eat, about what you're going to wear." Your Father, this gracious God, knows what you have need of. This gracious God made my heart and yours. God made this heart an addictive heart. God intends the heart to be addicted. The human heart has to be addicted to something. The trick is to get it addicted to the right thing, to wean it off its other addictions, which are spawned by insecurity, confusion, anxiety, and uncertainty.

Seek first God's reign, i.e. the sovereignty of the gracious God over your heart. Seek to be addicted to this God of ours. There is nothing this God of ours wants more than for us to be addicted with the addiction of love. And the parables we've mentioned, including the parable of the pearl and this teaching about seeking first the kingdom of God, these probably do not describe the present state of our hearts. They're descriptions of what we are to hope for and expect God will do in us if we will hope it. If we don't hope it, do we hope to hope it? And if we do, knock, ask, seek! God would have our hearts one, with one object of addiction, namely, God!

"Fear not little flock!" This comes after all these things God knows we have need of. We are told instead to seek the sovereignty of God, and all these things we have need of will come – all the things about which we have insecurity will come or they are already here. Therefore, "fear not little flock" (Luke 12:32).

For it is God's good pleasure to give us the kingdom – the kingdom being simply this experience of addiction to God as our wealth. This would presume we have a freedom in our hearts about our wealth so that we can sell our possessions and/or give alms. To provide ourselves with a purse that won't grow old, with a treasure that does not fail, where no thief approaches nor moth destroys. For where our treasure is, there our heart will be.

Singleness of heart has to do with knowing God as our wealth. Do we want that? Do we want the only way to integrity and the only source of it, which is God? If we want it – ask and seek and knock. If we don't want it, we need to deal with that lack of attraction in our prayer. Deal with that in your prayer honestly, and explain to God where you are.

Wealth Can Separate Us from the Love of God!

The good problem with wealth is that it makes so many of the wrong addictions possible. The problem is not wealth. The problem is that it facilitates so many addictions. So let us deal with where we are about our addictions, asking God to work on us and speak to us and grant us peace.

You'll learn more by resting your head on Christ's heart as John did (John 13:25) than by "figuring" because this matter of money is much, much more an emotional issue – having to do with fears and guilt and a lot of other "stuff" than with having to get it straight or clear. The head has an unbelievable capacity for leaving us immobile, requiring more and more information, but the heart walks toward truth, toward love.

Also, be careful trying to concoct a "theology of money," since in our intellectualizing we can miss the rather radical way that Jesus dealt with individuals in relationship to their possessions. Look at the differences in how He dealt with the rich young man and with Zacchaeus in Luke's Gospel. He never asked Zacchaeus for anything except dinner! Zacchaeus obviously wasn't married to his possessions. The rich young man must have, in his heart, thought he somehow was what he had.

His call is very different with each of us, and the timing is different with each of us. This is one of the reasons to be careful in making a universal principle out of something that is meant to be very personal; or making a generalization where the call is to a particular person at a particular moment in a personal walk with the Lord. Generalities are only good up to a point!

Lord, may this be a search in which we know in our hearts so much more about Your love of me and of us than about money. May that happen so that our use of resources, all of our resources, our eyes, our mouths, our talents, might serve You and delight you, and affect us in a way that is helpful in this walk that we have with You.

Questions from Session Participants

(See the Introduction for an explanation of the session format.)

First Question: You have said some things that confuse me. I understand the necessity to have a single heart toward God, but is it necessary to think in such either/or terms.

John Haughey: I'm clear that it is an either/or mind when it comes to possessions. "Fear not little flock, for it is your Father's good pleasure to give you the kingdom." Kingdom in this sense is a symbol of an abundance that comes from God. "Therefore, sell your possessions. . ." that you do not see and handle as coming from God in some way.

If it is the Father's pleasure to give you the kingdom which is abundance, the *pleroma* (a fullness that we receive from God; the counterpart of *pleonexia* the fullness that we seek to get for ourselves), then what you have now is to be seen as a promise and a beginning of a future abundance. So, the singleness has to do not with not having anything, but rather with valuing what you have as coming from and leading to union with God.

The single-purse symbol reminds us that it is your heart which assigns "worth": the worth of this, the worth of that, the worth of something else. From the heart comes the act of "worth-ship" – hopefully, the act of saying that the primary, primordial, fundamental worth of my life is God! So, all else is of secondary worth. All of my possessions can be turned into spiritual profit if put into the single purse that has assigned primary worth to God.

I think that's what makes a single heart. It is not that we end up with nothing. It's rather that all we end up with has worth in the light of the sovereignty of the Lord, the Christ, the Anointed One of God. This is not a big intellectual leap, but it is an awful discipline of the heart to make sure that there is nothing in my life that is functioning autonomously as its own sovereign, giving me orders that I obey, and then after that I obey God. No! All that I have is under the sovereignty of God. I take orders from that one Source because all of my wealth is in that single purse.

That is hard to grasp because we live in a culture where we have allowed the economy to be its own sovereignty. It keeps saying, "Obey the sovereignty of the economy." You can see what the sovereignty of the economy is doing to employees today in the era of downsizing. It's for us who know the absurdity of that sovereignty to act independently of it.

Second Question: You said that wealth is what makes our addictions possible, and so what we need is to become addicted to the love of God.

John Haughey: Yes, the heart is meant to be addicted. At least my heart has to be attached to something. My heart ain't making it alone. Is yours?

Third Question: Addiction has such a negative connotation, yet we are all compelled in this direction. It is such a complete switch for me to think about it the way you talk about it — the positive side of addiction. I am also struck by what you said about how wealth enables us to have all these addictions. One of the things I think wealth gives me is sort of an addiction related to having the time to attend this workshop, to study, etc. I have the freedom to take the time to do so many different things. However, to me, love and addiction are such different things.

John Haughey: Well, if you've ever been in love, you know you're addicted. So, I don't see them as different things. I think it's just the way the heart is. We have a little heart that was made for something other than itself. It is always going to be attached to something. Plural addictions make for diffuse spirits and faint faith and little or no "joy in the Lord."

Fourth Question: I found myself through my journaling coming down to one question and it was, Am I willing to come to God and dwell in God's presence when I might not get a "high" from it even though there is an alternative form which I think or feel I can get an immediate high? I'm not always going to feel something. I want to make God that number-one object of "worthship," but I need to be willing to not feel anything at times. The temptation for me when I'm not feeling something is to quick jump to one of these other things that I can get a quick "high" from.

John Haughey: I think that God loves us too much to have us confuse the consolations of God with the God of consolations. Meaning what? If the "get from" attitude is the only way I am attached to God, then God has the same problem that God had before, because it's the "give to" spirit rather than the "get from" spirit that will make us open to the length, the depth, the height, and the breadth of the Kingdom of God. The "give to" spirit makes a way for the prying open of this addicted heart so that it has room for something as high and tall and long and broad and deep as God.

9

The Spirit Is Willing, But . . .

Ignatius of Loyola has continued over the course of all my Jesuit years to teach me how to pray. Successful prayer for him presumed that you know what it is you're looking for when you enter into the period of prayer – what he calls the *id quod volo* – that which I want. If I know at least the ballpark I'm aiming to drop into, the prayer then ceases to be as meandering as prayer ordinarily is.

Since Ignatius suggests you have to ask the grace for a particular outcome or yield, the grace that I would ask for in this particular session is to better know what is robbing me of the experience of love that God has for me and the joy that Christ has won for me so that I can know the role that wealth is playing in my impoverishment. A document written by Mr. John Levy, entitled *Coping with Inherited Wealth,* comments on the problems that often accompany inheritance: "The inheritors suspect that their successes are the result of the wealth they have inherited. Many find it hard to be sure that they would be liked and respected if they had not had this affluence." There's also the lurking doubt that since I've never had to earn my living, could I? Like the butterfly that never develops adequately if it gets outside help in breaking out of its cocoon, many inheritors are spared their share of life's ordinary challenges.

People who have been protected by the comfort and seeming security that money provides, as Jung describes it, are wrapped in cotton. Their developmental processes have been truncated. A large inheritance can make it difficult to sustain an interest in or commitment to anything that requires intense and continuing effort, and the endurance of ambiguity, setbacks, and frustrations. Consequently, the goals of many whose experience is one of great inheritance is that their goals are not well defined nor strongly pursued.

Although many are driven to prove that they are capable, nevertheless their drives are frequently short-lived and not very intense. Boredom is a frequent experience. There is also guilt because it's often hard to accept unmerited good fortune. The guilt shows itself in many different ways, from one end of the behavioral spectrum to the other going through my life abjectly apologetic and on the other extreme, arrogantly contemptuous.

Those who inherit much when they're young feel different from their peers, and they frequently feel alienated as part of their psychic shape. Suspiciousness is also a frequent symptom. Gore Vidal identifies envy as *the* North American sin. He describes it as resenting the difference between another and myself, assuming that I can never get what the other has, maybe even desiring to bring the other down. The question develops: "Do people like me for me, or do they like me for what I have in order that they might get a piece of it?"

The way some people act toward the wealthy frequently has an obsequiousness to it, not to mention envy or resentment. There's something in the ethos of our North American culture which believes that a person who has enough money lives in a state of constant bliss. Consequently, the affluent who suffer are disbelieved or disdained. Evidence of or symptomatic of this is the media's delight in reporting the tribulations and foolishness of the rich. They're perceived and therefore treated as different from the rest of us.

One of the curses of poverty is that there aren't many options. Conversely, those who inherit much when they're young find that the plentitude of options often paralyzes them. One man is included in groups because he can pay for what the group plans. But he does not want to be included in groups simply for his ability to pay. He wants to be included for what he can do in the group – for his own talent, for his own abilities. The result is that rich people frequently play a kind of game where they act as if they aren't wealthy so they can be included as "just one of the folks."

These experiences of affluence constitute the *burden* of wealth. The question then is how to be free from that burden. What is it about the way Christ has saved us that is specific to the burden of affluence? I would subsume all those symptoms into one very heavy burden, the burden of *"sarx,"* a Greek word that is usually translated "flesh."

Paul's use of the word sarx is better understood as self-reliance, or self-sufficiency. *Autonomy* is the English word (from *autos nomos,* meaning self being the rule, self being the norm, self being the sovereign).

The fact is, I can come fairly close to self-sufficiency as an affluent person. I can come closer to self-sufficiency and self-reliance than others. So this temptation to being autonomous, which is endemic to being human, is a very severe temptation for those who can pay their way through much of what others have to work for and work hard at. It then becomes a spiritual problem because to the degree that I have come to exercise autonomous control in my life, I'm at a distance from the kind of dependency involved in having recourse to the Other who is God, the Other who is Christ.

The fact that I have so much going for me materially is very likely to secularize my worldview, limit my worldview, rivet my worldview to that which I can deal with and control in conditions which I can create or manipulate. The constant temptation for one whose experience is one of affluence is self-sufficiency.

"Flesh" should not be understood as sex or sin. That misses the point. But flesh, when it becomes the determinant of my life, leads to self-reliance, self-sufficiency, and on to self-indulgence. Therefore, we are warned in Galatians 5:16, "Do not live to gratify sarx, for the desires of sarx are against the Spirit and the desires of the Spirit are against sarx."

There is a war here between flesh and Spirit! They are opposed to each other. Flesh prevents you from doing what you in your better self want to do. This law of self-reliance is functioning in a way that is trying to get you to be autonomous, and it's lying to you! "But if you are under the Spirit, you are not under this law of sarx (self-reliance, self-sufficiency). But the fruit of living according to the law of the Spirit is love, joy, peace, kindness, goodness, faithfulness, gentleness, and self-control" (Galatians 5:18, 22-23). These are the fruit of living according to law of the Spirit – the nomos of the Spirit.

What are the consequences of living according to the nomos of sarx (the law of the flesh)? According to Galatians they are "immorality, impurity, licentiousness, idolatry, sorcery, enmity, strife, jealousy, anger, selfishness, dissension, party spirit, envy, drunkenness, carousing." It doesn't help relationships, you might say!

Autonomy always ends up isolating its aspirants. It's an offense against community. It renders community impossible. Sarx is certainly one of the driving forces of our culture. It shreds community and heightens individualism. Do your own thing! Do it *your* way!

I think of the man with the grain in Luke 12:16-21. He found he had a bumper crop and he was delighted. So he decided the best act of stewardship would be to build bigger barns to hold the grain. So far so good. Then he takes it easy, and he puts his feet up, and he says, "I have enough grain for eons. So eat, drink, and be merry!" He begins to think that his life and its continuance derive from what has made him affluent – the grain.

And, as the parable goes, "This very night your life shall be required of you." So he is named "fool" for having mistaken what he had going for him as the source of his life. There is never a sin associated with the man with the grain. There is just a failure in vision. The text keeps using the words "*my* grain" and "*my* barns" and "*my* wealth." His is the optic of a person whose life is ruled by sarx. His life is ruled by flesh. His life is ruled by that which flesh is able to produce. And there was no larger or deeper vision of the source of his wealth beyond the wealth itself.

The wealth made him a fool because he allowed it to delude him into thinking something that was false. It wasn't that his heart was addicted to the grain. It's that his mind was sarx saturated. Sarx is a principle of choice and it is contrasted in Paul's writings with *Pneuma,* that is, *Spirit.* Paul would say you can live according to the law of the Spirit or according to the law of the flesh. You're either autonomous or you're Spirit directed and he gives no third possibility, like both/and.

Sarx is not sin. Sarx is fallacy and blindness that leads to sin. It leads to misjudgment as the man with the grain misjudged the grain and therefore misjudged himself as having life through the grain. We start off thinking that we can do our own bidding with the grain and we end up doing the grain's bidding. With every single object of sarx that we buy into, we begin to be dictated to by it.

According to Paul in Romans 8:7-8, the mind that is set on flesh, that is the mind that is controlled by sarx – the mind that has as its principle of choice self-sufficiency, always ends up hostile to God. It does not submit to God. Those who live according to sarx cannot please God. And so, in domino fashion, one goes from sarx to sin to death. It seems that the reason why Jesus thinks that being rich is a dangerous condition to be in is because riches breathe the untruth that you can be self-sufficient. But there is no such thing as lasting self-sufficiency.

The only way wealth can profit one is to act on God's wealth with the mind of Christ. Then all of the injurious psychological consequences already cited that accrue to the affluent, it seems to me, would gradually begin to dissipate if the aspiration was not to get my act together, but together with God to act on God's wealth according to God's mind. The need to hear a clearer call about the disposition of wealth is very important, both psychologically and spiritually.

It would be good to look at two success stories about this whole thing of sarx, or self-reliance, that we have such a tendency to try to live by. The first story is the Zacchaeus story (Luke 19:1-10). "Jesus entered Jericho and was passing through that point and there was a man named Zacchaeus who was a chief tax collector and very rich."

There were two kinds of tax collectors, who were actually toll collectors. Toll booths were set up by the Romans across all the major roads in Palestine. Jericho was a key point for the tolls because Jericho came right at the point where those coming from Arabia up to or through Palestine would have to pass. As a chief tax collector, Zacchaeus basically stayed home and had his lesser tax collectors take the tolls. As chief tax collector, he was especially resented by the people because he figured out exactly what kind of tariff would be charged on the goods.

Since Zacchaeus became rich, people's resentment toward him isolated him. The townfolk had nothing to do with him because of his fraudulently acquired wealth. They thought he was as bad as, if not worse than, all the other tax collectors. Anyway, Zacchaeus sought to see Jesus with his own eyes but could not on account of the crowd because he was small of stature. So he ran on ahead and climbed into a sycamore tree in order to catch sight of Jesus, knowing He was to pass that way.

"And when Jesus came to the place, He looked up and said to him, 'Zacchaeus, make haste and come down, for I must stay at your house today.' So he made haste and came down and received Jesus joyfully. When the townspeople saw this they murmured, 'He has gone in to be the guest of a man who is a sinner.' And Zacchaeus stood and said to the Lord, 'Behold, Lord, half of my goods I give to the poor. And if I have defrauded anyone of anything, I restore it fourfold.' Jesus said to him, 'Today salvation has come to this house since he also is a son of Abraham. For the Son of Man has come to seek and to save the lost.' "

There are several things about this passage that I think are revealing about what robs us of our joy and deprives us of an awareness of God's love and about what, in fact, constitutes salvation. Let me land on the word "today" since it is used in three different places in this passage, e.g., "I must stay at your house today." The exegetes have an interesting analysis of "today" connected with salvation in the Gospel of Luke. In the first two Gospels, Matthew and Mark, these was a proximity to the historical happenings of Jesus of Nazareth. By the time we get to the third Gospel, Luke, we're up into at least the year 85. And the second coming of Jesus hasn't happened yet, as everyone expected it would by that time.

The question became, What is this kingdom – this salvation that is being postponed and postponed and postponed? The Christian community began to reflect on the postponement of this salvation that they awaited, and soon began to realize that it is in fact being experienced already, now, today in the joy that they had in their hearts, in the love of God that they had in their hearts, and through the love that they experienced with one another in community. This salvation is *not* postponed.

The salvation they were awaiting at the moment of the coming of God's Kingdom in glory is already here! The fruits of it are love of one another and an awareness that God is present among us here and now. So "today" in this passage about Zacchaeus begins to play a very enlightening function in the Gospel of Luke.

A second thing to note is the mix between rich and poor in the communities that was the immediate context for the Gospel of Luke. An awareness of the disparities between wealth and indigence in those communities grew, since the wealthy were beginning to turn to the Gospel. The particular problem that Luke had in mind, and one of His main reasons for writing the Gospel, was to deal with that disparity, i.e., the class disparity, wealth/indigence disparity. So this particular passage helps us become more aware that salvation is today, even as it shows that the evidence of being saved must also be today in the form of redistributions of wealth and doing justice in all our transactions.

Zacchaeus fills the bill. Zacchaeus says, "*Today,* I give half of my goods to the poor." That does not win him salvation, but it gives evidence of the change in his heart. "Not only do I give half my goods to the poor, but if I have defrauded anyone, I restore fourfold that which I have defrauded." So here is justice being done by Zacchaeus for the first time perhaps, at least in the perception of the community. This benevolence shown by Zacchaeus to the community wins two things. It wins his acceptance by the community, and it also gives evidence that in fact, his heart has undergone conversion. This is why Jesus says, "Today salvation has come to this house."

What would the behavior be like of a person who switched from living according to a sarx principle of discernment and choice, and began to live according to a Spirit principle? If the law of the Spirit became the source of his choice and discernment? Zacchaeus is a case in point. He would become a source of *benevolence* to the community in his relationship to them and to their poor. And he would be a source of justice in all his relationships by substituting fraud with a just return – not only a just return, but a fourfold form of justice.

The second story, Paul's "sarx-to-pneuma" conversion, is an even better example of a change in behavior. Paul's form of sarx was even more interesting than Zacchaeus's. He had taken measures to become the source of his own salvation through observance of the law. So he describes in clear terms the before and after picture as he moved *from sarx* as a principle of his activity *to Spirit* as a principle of his activity.

Phillippians 3:4-14 says, "Put no confidence in flesh (sarx). I myself have great reason for confidence in flesh, more reason than any of you. If any other person thinks he has reason for confidence in the flesh, listen to this: I was circumcised on the eighth day, I was of the tribe of Benjamin, I was a Hebrew born of Hebrews, as to the law,

I was a Pharisee, as to righteousness under the law, I was blameless. But whatever gain I had, I counted as loss now because of the surpassing worth of knowing Christ Jesus, my Lord. For His sake, I have suffered the loss of all things and count them as so much refuse in order that I may gain Christ and be found in Him. Not having a righteousness of my own that has accrued to me through flesh observing law, but a righteousness that is based on faith in Christ Jesus, a righteousness from God that depends on faith that I might know Him and the power of His resurrection; and may share His sufferings, becoming like Him in His death."

Now essentially, he says, "I'm not bragging about this. I'm telling you that in this new life I'm living I don't have my act together! I am not perfect, but what I am doing is pressing to make it my own because Christ has made me His own." "One thing I do, forgetting what lies behind and straining forward to what lies ahead, I press on toward the goal for the prize of the upward call of God in Christ Jesus" (Phillippians 3:13-14).

So we have a Zacchaeus and his changeover and a Paul and his changeover. We also have the fact that all who have been baptized into Christ Jesus have the capacity to make the changeover. But it's always a free choice. We may *not* want to live according to the law of the Spirit. We may *prefer* to live according to the law of the flesh. And if we live according to the law of the flesh, we've got no place to go but toward joylessness, toward hostility with one another, and toward death in sin.

If we choose to live according to this new principle which is already in us, we can know the joy of the Master, we can hear the word of the Master – the word of the Master spoken to us that His joy might be in us and our joy might be complete.

Then we can get on with the task of being stewards –
first of the mysteries of God housed in us and then by
material acts of stewardship – disposing of the property
of the Master according to the mind and the heart of the
Master. We can, of course, so easily become self-indul-
gent using the property of the Master – squandering it
for purposes other than the ones for which it was given
us. We need the grace to better know what is robbing us
of the joy and the experience that God would have us
live in, and to know the role that wealth is playing and
might play in this.

For Reflection

How am I dealing with my desires for self-sufficiency, self-
reliance, autonomy?

Is the experience of Zacchaeus or Paul foreign to me? If
so, do I aspire to it?

10

Suffering's Value/Loyalty's Value

In the last session I covered the meaning of *sarx* and *pneuma* because it seems to me we'd be playacting at being stewards of the Master's property (which wealth is), if the interior principle of activity that was moving us was self-reliance and self-sufficiency – in a word, sarx.

An autonomous steward is a contradiction in terms. You can't be managing the Master's property as a steward and living a heart life, a mind life, a norm life independently of the Master. A sarx-directed steward, one who seeks to be self-sufficient and self-reliant, won't be a steward very long because he'll be interested in making his own way.

That having been said, we're up against an almost impossible situation because there's no one in the room, I suspect, who is not attempting to live self-reliantly and self-sufficiently. Which brings us to that moment in the life of the hearers of Jesus when they were exasperated with His words and ways. It was after the rich young man turned away that Jesus said, "How hard it is for those who have riches to enter into the Kingdom of God. It's easier for a camel to go through the eye of a needle than for the rich man to enter the Kingdom of God." Those who heard Him complained, "Then who can be saved?" And He said that what is impossible with your own resources is possible with God (Luke 18:24-26).

So let us pray: We have been examining the aspiration to be God-reliant which You, Lord, have put in our hearts, which we are far from realizing. All we can do is lay the seeming impossibility of accomplishing it on Your doorstep and promise only that we will desire it, pray for it, knock on the door of your power for it, until it comes true. And You will have done it in us. Self-sufficiency is so much a part of our culture and our hearts that the very idea of being reliant on You, surrendering to You, losing our footing in You, is not natural to us. Which is why we make this prayer through Christ the Lord.

One of the values of personal suffering is that self-sufficiency and self-reliance break down. You know that from your suffering; and you know that as the suffering increases, so the reliance on God increases, and that's to the good. I'm going to assume for now that your experience and understanding of that is in place and move to another point.

This second point is the value of the suffering of others. What is the mind of the Master, whose property I manage, about the suffering of others? How am I to see their suffering in relationship to the wealth the Master has put at my disposal? What is the mind of the Master about their suffering in relationship to my resources?

For the Master, sufferers were like so many sacraments. It's very revealing; those who touched their suffering were touched by God for doing so. Those who touched the sufferings of others in the Gospels achieved a wholeness that they otherwise were not able to achieve. For those who think they have it together, those who don't have it together can be a source of truth and grace, and even the beginning of the end of a futile self-sufficiency, not to mention the beginning of a God-composed kind of integrity. Several texts to make the point:

> "There was a very rich man (Dives) who was dressed
> in purple and linen and feasted splendidly every day.
> At his gate lay a beggar named Lazarus who was cov-

ered with sores and who longed to eat the scraps that
fell from the rich man's table." (Luke 16:19ff.)

The rich man didn't have a clue about the role that Lazarus could play in his life until they both died. From his
place of torment and flames, the rich man pleads with
Abraham, who is on the other side of the great abyss, an
abyss fixed by the rich man's choice, to have Lazarus
come to dip the tip of his finger in water to refresh his
tongue.

There's a great reversal here. What had appeared to
be merely indigence in Lazarus, as it turned out, was coupled by an unseen richness, namely the predilection of
God and Abraham for him. And what had appeared to be
merely affluence in the rich man was coupled by an un-
suspected indigence – a terminal interior impoverishment. The rich man's affluence enabled him to enjoy a
virtually impregnable autonomy. His affluence created in
him an illusion of having it together. The suffering of
Lazarus could have broken into this illusion and reversed
the engines. Dives could have come to understand his
own poverty. By touching the sores of Lazarus, he could
have been relieved of some of his own resources, the excess of which blinded him to the poverty that he actually
lived in. Instead he chose to remain detached, self-en-
closed, uninvolved, in a word – autonomous. The point
here has to do with the implications of the value for
Dives of Lazarus's suffering and poverty.

A God-composed integrity can begin to develop in
the rich through the poor who are in need of a portion
of the Master's property. A life of union with God, a spiritual life, a life which has the other as a focus, can begin
whether the other is a big *O* or a little *o*.

Another text that whacks us over the head with the
same point is Matthew 25:31, where those who are wel-

comed into the Kingdom by the Son of God are those who took in the stranger, and clothed the naked, and fed the hungry. Why were they welcomed in when they didn't know the theological and religious value of the actions they were performing? Because the One for whom they were performing them was the Son of Man Himself.

A third text, which is also key here (Luke 10:25-37), is about the lawyer who wants to know how he can come to this God-composed integrity, which he calls eternal life. There is a discussion about "who is my neighbor" and we know the story, we've heard many times about the fellow who is violently handled and left by the side of the road. The Levite goes by; the priest goes by; the irreligious Samaritan goes by and because he could deflect his own agenda, deplete his own resources – the mule, the oil, the wine, the silver pieces – he's the one who stands to inherit eternal life.

In the course of letting in the little *o*, the little other, who was violently treated by society, and acting compassionately on his behalf, the Samaritan inherits eternal life. His autonomy yielded to another. And he made use of the Master's property even though he didn't know it was the Master's property. And he used the Master's property according to the mind of the Master – and hence the God-composed integrity of eternal life received, i.e., he inherited eternal life.

So, we have two cases here of the little *o*'s whose sufferings can bring others to the kind of integrity that moves from sarx to pneuma – that becomes *God* reliant. A fourth text is a little more uncomfortable. It's Luke 14:12-13. Jesus is saying here, if you could accept my words, that one certain way for people to become mired in that posture of soul which is self-reliant and self-sufficient, is to socially reinforce one another in that particular condition of soul. Jesus is saying in Luke 14:12, I'd like to suggest that you have hardened your sensibilities. Your autonomies have become reinforcing of one another. There's a social fixity to them. I'd suggest, therefore, that instead of inviting your friends or your brothers and sisters or your relatives or your wealthy neighbors to your lunches and your dinners, you think of inviting the beggars and the crippled and the lame and the blind and the smelly and the discourteous.

Initiate a colleagueship with those who are marginalized to your form of sociability and are in fact marginal to society. Why? Because they can't repay you. To repay only reinforces you in this posture of self-reliance that you live in. Most of our table companions are paybacks. This would mean that one is not likely to break out of the company of those trying to be invulnerable, the autonomous, those who have it made, those who can return the favor, those who've got it together. Solidarity, on the other hand, with the "losers" of this world can only help one to an appreciation of the truth of one's own vulnerability. The only repayment one can have from such people is to be reminded of one's own fragility, powerlessness, and vulnerability – which is no small repayment.

Jesus has this eschatological statement – "Know that you'll be repaid in the resurrection of the *just*" (Luke 14:14). And who will be our companions in the resurrection of the just? Those who use and receive the property of the Master according to the mind of the Master. What is the mind of the Master? To redistribute God's wealth according to human need.

Then somebody breaks into the conversation and says, "Happy is the one who eats bread in the Kingdom of God" (Luke 14:15), which makes Jesus move into another statement that is even more uncomfortable (Luke 14:16-22). "I'd like to describe the future to you. I'd like to describe the future banquet to you," He says. In effect, "It's going to be attended by the poor and the crippled and the blind and the lame," the very ones He had mentioned before as those you should be bringing into your house – from the highways and the hedgerows. Whereas you who were preoccupied by their affairs, having bought several yoke of oxen, having bought some fields, and who had to decline the invitation to the banquet because you were otherwise preoccupied – not one of you will taste a morsel of this banquet.

What disqualified them? They disqualified themselves. They couldn't be bothered. It didn't attract them. They didn't need it. They were otherwise preoccupied. When the invitation came, they declined it.

And what qualified the rest of them? Precisely that they *didn't* have it together; precisely because they hadn't eaten a good meal in some time; precisely because an invitation from someone to someplace was alien to their experience but related to their needs. Since their needs were unmet, they were still looking, still waiting, still needing a fullness that was future to them, foreign to them, and beyond them. This in contrast to those who were already full! Woe to those who are already full! (Luke 6:24).

There is great value in our own suffering as well as in others' sufferings with respect to the very subjects we've been talking about. Sufferings bring us up short about the mind of the Master, about the property of the Master. And the mind of the Master about His property is (among other things): My property is for all people. To be My steward you must be a people-sensitive person because that's what My property is for. And of all the people that My property is for, the one I have the greatest fondness for is the one who is least among you. Furthermore, I would touch you through them and bring you to the wholeness that you strive for – through them!

At dinner tonight I got into a conversation that makes me add a footnote – one that I'm *not* totally comfortable with since I am not a parent and I have no money! But it seemed to those of us at dinner that it was worth bringing up even though it's complex. It has to do with the little *o's* that are your children and the wealth of the Master in relationship to those little *o's*. More specifically, when is withholding the inheritance a greater act of love for your children than bequeathing the inheritance to them? Or conversely, when is a greater suffering impeded by withholding their inheritance from them? Ever? So the discussion matured a bit along these lines.

What was family to Jesus? What place did family play in the mind of the Master? It seemed like a lot of the quotes from the lips of the Master in the New Testament are tough on family – starting when Jesus, at twelve years of age, stayed behind in the temple. Then as He goes into His public ministry, it seems like He's often trying to lure His hearers away from lesser loyalties – like loyalties to the temple, to the law, and to family. He's trying to win them into deeper loyalties and into the new family, which was not born of flesh and blood but by water and the Spirit. He crashes into family loyalty with all kinds of upsetting statements: "Anyone who loves mother and father more than Me is not worthy of Me" (Matthew 10:37). Or in response to "Master, I'll follow you wherever You go, but first I have to bury my father" – "Follow Me and let the dead bury the dead" (Luke 9:59-60). Heavy, heavy! James and John are in the boat fixing up the nets of the old man. He summons them and they jump out of the boat, abandoning their father then and there and going off in Jesus' company.

What was wrong with family that He was so tough on it? Well, it took twenty centuries for us to come up with some of the answers, and the answers are better known by you than by me. How much of the dysfunction of modern life comes from what has been scripted in the heads of children – about who they are and what's expected of them and how they will win self-esteem, etc. No one doubts the particular burdens of growing up in a family of enormous inheritance. The fact is that almost all adult dysfunction is traceable to family. We can't do without family, but why is Jesus leery about statements that are simply pro-family?

It seems to me that Jesus saw a whole nation of people whose loyalties made them unavailable to obey God or follow Him. He preached an in-breaking Kingdom of God and found relatively few followers. He preached and poured out a new wine, which they insisted on catching in old wineskins. Could it be that one of the reigning idolatries in the hearts of Jesus' hearers was family? Not family as such, but family as a locus so often of accommodation and compromise, of codependency and irresponsibility, of myopia and insularity. Could it be that what Jesus saw was not love of family member for family member, but group self-reliance?

His own family that He grew up with was appalled by Him. They were so appalled that one day they went out to fetch Him home because they were sure He had gone mad, as Mark says. And when He went back to the place of family in Nazareth, He couldn't work any miracles because they put Him in the old wineskins of the carpenter's son: "we know His brothers and sisters!" So He shook the dust off His feet and went elsewhere. Could it be that we've accommodated or ignored this very radical attitude of Jesus toward family in order to fit into categories that have not been converted by Him?

To seek first the Kingdom of God and God's justice; to love God with our whole heart, soul, mind, and strength is very radical stuff! One of the themes that cuts across this theme of family, as He treats it, is the eschatology that's going on in the Gospels. "I'm creating a new family – a new family composed of people who have left all to follow Me. I give you My word, there's not anyone who has given up home, brothers, sisters, mother, father, children, property for Me and for the Gospel who will not receive in this present age a hundred times as many homes, brothers, sisters, mother, father, children, and property and in the age to come everlasting life."

Could it be that one of the reasons why our churches are so effete is because we insist upon holding on to blood family rather than Spirit family, the family born from above? How often do we try to make blood family our actual treasure – the pearl of great price where our treasure is located?

It's not that Jesus was anti-family; He was suprafamily. Not having a family, that's all very easy to talk about. Having families and having wealth, I leave it to you to talk about – fully aware that it's a loaded, loaded subject. So don't blame it on me. Blame it on the people that were at the table this evening and this radical way we try to follow and understand Jesus, first of Nazareth and now seated at the right hand of the Father.

Question: I keep wrestling with the notion you articulated – "among all my people, the ones I have the greatest fondness for are the least among you." Could you say more about that?

John Haughey: I can only say what Jesus said. When did we see you this way (homeless), that way (hungry), another way (a stranger)? When you did this or that service to those who were in an indigent condition, you were doing that to Me. The one part of the church that has picked up on this theme and has deepened it and created a powerful reflection on it, is the Latin American church. The particular words they prefer are "preferential option for the poor." The point they make is that God has a predilection for them.

Same Participant: "Why couldn't that be explained in your first sentence – that the mind of the Master is to redistribute the wealth according to human need, and the preferential option for the poor is because that's where the need lies and that's why that is the preferred option, not because He is more for those people but because the need is greater?"

John Haughey: Well, I think the one doesn't exclude the other, and I think there is scriptural warrant for both from the texts I took. Little Lazarus and his little sores could have bridged the chasm, had the rich man chosen to make the move. But it was the rich man's gate that was locked, and Lazarus got up to the gate and that's as far as he could get. That's where it stopped because the rich man chose to have it stop there. I'm not imagining the redemptive importance of the suffering for the rest of us of those in need. I'm citing it, and that's what is so uncomfortable.

And while I'm at it, let me end with a caveat against overly simplistic ways of taking this whole theme as in the Samaritan story: "I have to postpone my agenda – in order to take care of the person that I saw on my way to work – where I was in fact going to set up or fund or participate in the process of a low-income housing project that involved 237 units." It doesn't mean you always divert your attention from the many to the one. But it does mean that your resources – your mental resources, your physical resources, your financial resources – are for the sake of others, the needs of others rather than only your own needs or those of that little unit of which you are a part. You reinforce one another in a worldview that is short of Gospel while perhaps mouthing Gospel. That doesn't always mean taking in the one, but it always means that the purpose of the property of the Master is people and their dignity and whatever reinforces their dignity.

The reason why this is more complex right now is because we're increasingly aware of the dependency problem, when some resources simply go ignorantly to meet human need and create dependency and in fact don't reinforce dignity. So we're more sophisticated about that, but in the course of being more sophisticated about that, I think we're pulling away from the compassion that is much more primary – and is essential for Christianity.

So it's not an invitation to an oversimplification about human need. It's an invitation to say – however it all works and notwithstanding all the complexity and all the learning that has to go into it – property is for people! The property I have disposition over is for people! That's the mind of the Master, however that shakes out.

How to go about this would entail a different response for everybody because their angle of vision, their call, their grace would be different. So I'm talking about a principle. I'm not saying how the principle ought to take shape for you personally. There should be response by you to call, not response to an idea or to being cajoled by guilt.

For Reflection

Where am I with the wisdom that comes from suffering? What have I learned from this source?

Where am I with the issues voiced about the inheritance that is to accrue to our children? Is that something less than love of them?

11

A Conversation about the Poor and Wisdom Partners

John Haughey: I thought that rather than introducing new matter here, it might be good to talk about some of the seeds that have begun to sprout as a result of your conversations with one another, your hearing of the word the Lord is speaking to you, and as a result of new understandings. I thought it might be better to begin to reap, possibly prematurely, that which has been sown.

Participant: "Could you say something about the kingdom, as something only children can enter, and growth in wisdom?"

John Haughey: I like the dialectic that you give – the need to be impulsive as a child, trusting as a child, joyful as a child, and not carrying the "curse of adulthood" around with us. The other side of it is a needed wisdom that we don't ordinarily associate with children – the wisdom that comes through experience. I think one of the ways of making sure that the impulse is not impulsiveness is to have a person that we are in dialogue with. It may be too formal to call the person a spiritual director because that sounds more formal. I'm speaking of a person whose perception of wisdom we really trust and to whom we can open ourselves up, to test our impulses in order to know, from the perceived wisdom of that other person, whether an impulse is guilt or whether it is God or whether it's crazy or whether it's prudent.

So, I think a partnership, maybe even a partnership with a spiritual director – let's call it a "wisdom partner" – is a helpful thing. "Where two or three are gathered in My name," the Lord is more likely to be than where one, ungathered, keeps hearing things.

Participant: From her experience at the Church of The Savior Community, Dorothy Devers has written a book called *Faithful Friend.* She had trouble with that term "spiritual director" and wanted to meet that concern. It is a pamphlet-type book that is available at the Potters House Bookservice in Washington, D.C. This book is written to show how the benefit of a mutual relationship and not just one seeking the wisdom of another person.

John Haughey: It may be an especially important relationship for those of you who have this burden of considerable wealth that we've been talking about this weekend, because as you know from the companionship that you've found here, this is a very difficult area to have clear discernment about. We talked about the amount of emotion that's connected to the "boodle" that we have. That emotion makes discernment difficult. This trusted wisdom figure helps keep the emotion minimal as one seeks to make prudent choices. If I'm going to hear a call, I follow it. In the course of following it, I need somebody to test the call and the reality of my following. That's the function of the wisdom partner.

Participant: We've gotten our wealth through an economic system that we feel oppresses a large number of people. That seems to imply a special responsibility as to what we do with it. How do you fit this fact and these concerns into the God-centered approach we've taken this weekend?

John Haughey: I have three comments about that. The first is that those who are marginal to the system clarify to those who are its beneficiaries what is dysfunctional about the system.

So I think that valuable, even profound, social analysis often comes from friendship with those who are least benefited by the system. And when I say friendship, I don't mean just doing a good act for someone, but really being one with that person, so you begin to see exactly how the system is dysfunctional from the bottom up. If what is dysfunctional about the system comes best through friendship with those who hurt the loudest about its dysfunction, then "With whom do I have lunch?" is not an insignificant concretization of the issue.

The second comment I want to make is that the system can reduce each person in it to 30 pieces of silver. The term for that particular kind of analysis is economism. Economism takes seriously only those who can pay for the services of the system. Any system that works economistically has got to have more evil than good in it because the criterion for choice and decision and policy and program in that system is going to be monetary, not personal.

The third comment: I think what loving the marginal person will do is begin to stoke fire in your belly. And then I think you have to go from a relationship with your friend to a passionate concern about the particular policies, or their absences, that denigrate or ignore him or her. There is a direct continuum from those with whom you have in-depth friendship who are marginal to the system, to the efforts we take to change its policies. But you can't stop at one. It has to move to the other.

Participant: I wonder if you could say something about the role of repentance in terms of dealing with the sarx principle.

John Haughey: Sarx is a principle of activity that leads to sin. The root meaning of repentance in the Hebrew means to turn around from inside, so that I face into a different horizon. The problem with the horizon that sarx looks at is it is confined to the empirical and to that which concerns my interests. As confined to that which is of self-interest, it's a horizon that opens out into falsehood. Repentance turns to a horizon that both awaits and experiences the in-breaking Kingdom of God.

So repentance is a turnaround, a repugnance for the world that was confined by my own self-interest, and my attraction to the new creation that is in-breaking. This is not a world of self, but of solidarity with my brothers and sisters, since the Kingdom of God is a social reality. So repentance is the move from a confined self toward solidarity, from sarx to pneuma.

The problem with the world of sarx is it doesn't have room for God. It eventually becomes irritated with the divine, as you saw in the parable of the tenant farmers – "What the hell is he doing coming in here asking for the grapes? We're doing fine, thank you! Get rid of him!" He reminds us of a different horizon, and we can't tolerate the reminder. Repentance is that move which involves sorrow for the sin of working within a horizon which was too small for me, too little for us. Repentance brings me out to glimpse the length and breadth and height and depth of the vision God intended in making my heart as big as it is, not withstanding all my experiences of how cribbed, cabined, and confined it can get.

Participant: Could you make some comments on Jesus' statements about the poor being with us always? Does this statement relate to what we've been talking about here?

John Haughey: The reason the poor will always be with us is because we *are* the poor. The value of those who are experiencing their vulnerability is to remind the rest of us who might be ignoring our vulnerability that vulnerability is the middle name of every human being. The fragility of mortality is endemic to the human condition. It won't go away – which means we need a Lord, we need a Savior, and it will never be other than that. And the actual poorest of the poor among us are those who don't know who. As long as you own your poverty, you'll need a Lord and Savior – you'll need a sovereign that's not yourself. Sarx is its own sovereignty and that's why it leads to sin, and why it always leads to hostility toward God.

Participant: I came here feeling it was possible to figure some things out, and you referred in your prayer to the impossibility of solving this problem ourselves. That's been one of the great insights for me this weekend – that this is something I can't figure out. The image that came to my mind was that of a child with a knot in his shoe coming to his parent to get it out. I related this to God being the one who is capable of untying the knot – not that we're not involved somehow – but there are aspects to this that only God can handle. I felt real hope in Jesus' words that with man it is impossible, but with God it *is* possible to deal with these issues of wealth.

John Haughey: I like that! Let me just put that in even a different context. The great insight of the Latin Americans about how the truth comes, I've really savored. How does the figurer come to the place of figuring with clarity? The insight of the liberation theologians is that truth comes up through your feet and then it comes into your head – or it comes in through your hands and then it comes into your head. When you *do* the little bit that you see, you *see* more as a result of the little that you do.

In liberation theology there is the world of praxis (that is the world of *do*) and there is the world of theory – and there is always a dialectic. The knowing comes from the doing of the truth and then the knowing comes back into the doing. Praxis is always enlightened doing. There is a dialectic in which action and theory play off each other. The action is taken on the theory that was developed from the action previously taken.

Now the western way of working it is first you know, first you see, first you understand, and then you do. I think the Latins got it right. In matters of money, you will only know the truth you do.

Participant: I just want to underline the understanding that it is impossible to work out our money issues in an abstract form in isolation from the poor. Since we've come to live (as a family) in Adams Morgan (area of Washington, D.C.), we've had this incredibly rich yet appalling experience of continually being confronted by the homeless and by people with polystyrene cups bumping us in the stomach as we walk down the street. It's been an incredible experience for us. For me, it's been the lived-out discovery of what Jesus says in Matthew 25:31ff., which has always been a challenge for me. When somebody asks who Jesus is, He says I *am* the homeless. He doesn't say I'm *like* a homeless person (He's not metaphorical). He's saying that's who I am.

So I don't go out to *help* the poor so much as I go out to be converted by them. I go out to deepen my own conversion – Jesus is really there! If I'm trying to meet Jesus in a textbook or in theological discussions, that's really just preparatory work. It's in the actual doing – of walking, of touching, of seeing that I meet Jesus and am converted.

The particular story I'd like to share is about the evening my wife and I were just walking down 18th Street in Washington, D.C., and we saw this little black man walking beside people. He was serenading them. For the most part people would ignore him. He tended to choose couples. In a sense there was a real gift in what he was doing for them because he had a beautiful voice. And they would keep on walking down the road and he would just be smiling at them, serenading, and he would walk about 100 yards and if they hadn't given him any money, he'd say good-bye. He'd walk back up the street the other way with another couple.

So we and the two children were there and we went and talked to him. We had this incredible conversation that went on for a long time. Sometime in the dialogue, he had this story about his being homeless for about a year and a half.

There was an extraordinary buoyancy in this man. He said that he was a Christian and what a wonderful privilege it was for him to be on the streets. And he really sensed that God was blessing him very deeply. Then he said, "To whom much is given, much is expected." And he was talking about himself! He meant it. He felt this great responsibility. He felt that God had really given him this experience so that he would be able to minister to his brothers and sisters on the street. When he said, "To whom much is given, much is expected," I *knew* that I was hearing the Gospel. I knew I was hearing what God wanted me to hear. That's my continual experience on the streets of Adams Morgan. I suppose my tears here are a symbol of that. So, it's impossible to work it out in isolation. This is what makes it all tangible.

John Haughey: If you do the truth you know, you'll come to know what you are called to do. If you don't take the steps into the truth you know, you'll never know what you're called to do. Truth comes in the darnedest places, where you don't expect it. So you have to make yourself available to it. This image of the in-breaking Kingdom is an image of coming into truth. And God would speak truth to us much, much more than we care to hear it. But the speaking will become remote when we do not act on what we have already heard.

Participant: This just brings me back to one of the most helpful things that Mother Teresa said to me, at least, when I was with the group over there – that she doesn't do anything great, she just does small things with great love. That brings spirituality back to the possible for me. If I can bring it back into that small thing and be willing to do that, then the promise of knowing the truth and hearing better the call is a hopeful thing.

John Haughey: A text that would be appropriate and that especially appeals to me: "I will show you a still more excellent way. . . ." (the last verse of 1 Corinthians 12, and following). If I were to do extraordinary things – speak in the tongues of angels, understand all mysteries and all knowledge, give all I have away – and have not love, it's a "nothing burger." So Mother Teresa's statement is an important statement!

We do little things with as much love as we can muster. The "boodle" will disappear, but love never ends. What of what I have lasts? Nothing of what I *have* lasts. What of what I *do* lasts? That which is done in love lasts. Love never fails!

"Now we see in a mirror dimly, but then face to face. Now I know in part. Then I will understand fully, even as

I am fully understood. So faith, hope, and love abide, and the greatest of these is love. Make *love* your aim."

Participant: I have placed so much emphasis in my life on planning, strategizing, and goal setting. I find myself gravitating toward these out of a pleasure in the process. Some things recently have have caused me to churn inside, and yet this need to be organized, appear responsible, etc., is so strong in me. So I feel this great conflict between what I'm feeling in this churning and what I illustrate in my planned, controlled exterior. So I get tied up in knots and feel that if these knots can be undone, my love can be so much more extensive.

John Haughey: It's humble of you to put it that way. It resonates in my own heart too, both about my own life and in my area of understanding. I think one of the reasons why integrity attracts me is that there is a continuum between what is inside with what is outside. The flow is key, and the particular temptation I have that I resonate with you about is trying to get it all together in my head. It doesn't get together in your head! How does the Magnificat go? "He has confused the proud in their hearts" (Luke 1:51). You can get confused if you try to get it together in your head. Once again, if you *act* on the truth you know, then it gets together outside yourself and then comes back into a deeper comprehension.

Participant: I would like to come back to a passage that I think we really need to come to terms with. It is the passage where the woman showered her love on Jesus in an extravagant anointing and the disciples, in response, reacted with indignation. Why this waste when the ointment could have been sold and given to the poor? Jesus responded that the poor you; always have with you, you do not always have Me.

I believe that the point that Jesus was making was "The poor you have with you all the time. How is it that you never become indignant on their behalf except when you see money wasted on me? You don't always have me before your eyes. The poor you *always* have before your eyes. It's curious that you're only indignant when the money is expended on Me."

I have decided I must be indignant on behalf of the poor at *all* times, not only when money is given to the church to buy a $40,000 organ or something.

John Haughey: I work with a lot of groups, but there is something about this group that is "off the wall," and I mean that *not* in the "California sense," but it's just a beautiful group! In a sense, we just got going. May the Lord bring us all into greater truth by doing the truth we come to know in love.

12

Sabbathing Revisited

When I was a kid I used to like to listen to Jack Benny on the radio. I remember how much of a cheapskate he was. On one program a mugger comes up to him and says, "Your money or your life!" And Benny doesn't say anything for a while. The mugger says, "Well?" Benny replies, "Don't rush me. I'm thinking!"

I'm presently thinking – not about my money or my life – but about what your input has been about your expectations. I'd say the room is divided in half. That is, I hear two different kinds of expectations. One kind of expectation is, "I need more information about wealth and its use. I need more knowledge." Therefore, the expectation is that this weekend is going to be one of more information and more knowledge. I'm not unhappy with that except that's not what we'd best be doing.

I think there will be a lot of information during the course of the weekend – coming from me and coming from you, maybe more you than me. But again, I think what we're primarily doing here is something different from that.

Each of you is in a different situation with respect to money. You all have a different relationship to it and you all have different emotional attitudes toward it. You've heard the emotions – some of them positive, some of them negative. A lot of ambiguity, a lot of tension, a lot of questions about what money is doing to your relationships or could do to them.

I think the more important thing to stress is not information but for you to take your relationship to wealth and your relationship to God and in the course of the weekend, hear in your heart what God would say to you about the connection between the two.

I come from a spiritual tradition which believes that if you want to hear God's word spoken to you specifically and unmistakably, there are disciplines that will enable you to hear that word. It's on the basis of that experience and that spirituality that I make this distinction between being more informed (and there is no end to the need to be more informed, and to be more informed about money is a good thing) and listening in your own heart to what God would say to you.

If there are 35 of us in this room, there will be 35 different messages if each of you wants to hear the one for you. Rather than going home with a lot of different ideas, listen for God's words spoken to you from within and for your own emotional response to them. Getting some ideas about money is not the deepest value of the weekend; not the best use of the weekend; not the deepest purpose of the weekend.

So I want to clear the air about this right away and ask whether you would make an act of faith in God's ability to speak personally to you about your relationship to others, self, and God and about your relationship to your financial resources. This is key for our time together. Otherwise we could have a lot of interesting conversations together, but I don't know what the value of these would be because you are called personally by God at least in part through the medium of the resources you have going for you.

I have no idea what your call is. I haven't a clue. You would not be well served by me if I did because I'd put a "trip" on you. You don't need a trip. I could put a trip on you about the poor, for example. You don't need that. That would disserve your relationship to God. That disserves the uniqueness of each of our relationships to God.

I really found a remarkable series of statements coming out of you. I wrote every one of them down. I've been fascinated by this whole thing of what money does to character, what money does to the soul, what money does to love, what money does to power, what money does to one's self-sense. When I was 19 years old I took a perpetual vow of poverty, and I have not wanted for anything since. Nor do I own anything. So I look at your tensions about this issue in a sense from afar. I will share with you the methods I have learned for hearing God. That is the best thing I can do on your behalf.

Rather than go through all of the statements, let me just land on one. It was one that Vicky made: "I came here to be emptied enough to hear a clear word." That sums up why I think we are right to have silence, and Scripture, and thoughtful conversation with one another.

There is a value in getting to know one another, but the specific purpose of our sharing is in relation to hearing the unique word that God would say to each of us. Who knows where it will come from? It may come from Scripture. It may come from personal prayer. It may come from small group. It may come right out of the blue into your heart. It may come after the weekend is over and you reflect and distill and conclude, "That seems right."

The style of the weekend that I would like to recommend is that it be a sabbath – a sabbath in the ancient Jewish sense of the word that was a time to be use-less. It is not a time to be working. It is not even a time to be thinking but a time to be feeling – a time to be a child. The purpose of sabbath is rest. Every seventh day, the whole Jewish community and each person were to rest as God rested on the seventh day in order to enjoy all the good things that happened on the previous six days. One of the purposes of sabbath was to learn to be a child again; to not be in control but to be taken care of the way a child is by a parent. I'd like to suggest that the style for this weekend should be seen in terms of sabbath.

Sabbath has a lot to do with being quiet inside yourself. If you know yourself very well, you know it takes a while to quiet down. You can't go straight from hubbub to silence to quiet. You often have to go from silence to turbulence to quiet. Then in quiet you begin to listen better because you hear from a deeper place.

Again, I'd like to suggest that a sabbath kind of weekend could equip you to be cared for by the goodness of God. Let yourself praise God, thank God, and love God. Let yourself be found by God. Yours is a freedom from having to do anything so that from a deeper place in yourself you can hear the word that God would say. That word may be about money. It may well not be about money. It may be about you. It may be about your spouse. It may be about your children or neighbor. It may be a word of comfort. It may be a word of correction. It may be a word of clarification. It may be a word you heard before and didn't act on. That's quite likely.

The anthropology and the spirituality of the thing are the same. God wants to say something at this point in your relationship, at this point in your discipleship with Christ. What is it that God would say to you?

The best prayer you can say this weekend is the prayer of petition: "Lord, what would you have me hear? What would you have me do? Who would you have me be? What would you have me become?"

Out of the depth of that simple prayer you will be spoken to. At least that has been my experience in every single encounter I've ever had with God and every single encounter I've been asked to direct or oversee with anybody. If you want to hear what God would say to you, God will have something to say to you. Silence is important and silence is not just the absence of words. It is letting myself get past the turbulence; to put myself in a desert where I begin to thirst and know what I am thirsting for. I will begin to ask for living water.

For desired outcomes of the weekend I would suggest three. (I don't thereby dismiss the expectations each of you had, but let me just present these to you if you want to entertain them as possible outcomes.)

The Scripture for tomorrow in most of our churches that really impressed me is one line from Acts 9:31. As you know, the Acts of the Apostles is a description of the state of the church being born and as it went through its fledgling moments. So we get to Acts 9:31 – "Then the church throughout all of Judea and Galilee and Samaria had peace and was being built up; and walking in the fear of the Lord and in the comfort of the Holy Spirit it grew."

Very interesting to me are the connections being made here. The fear of the Lord is not a dread nor a paralysis but an awe thing, a wonder thing, a wow thing, a "look at what God is doing!" thing. Growth in the fear of the Lord is growth in awareness of God, in alertness about what God is doing. I'm seeing God at work in this or that person and I'm awed! I get more and more awed by the work of God. There is growth in the fear (awe) of God coupled with growth in comfort – the comfort of the Holy Spirit; the consolation of the Holy Spirit; the continual being tinctured with joy by the Spirit of God touching my heart; touching our hearts in the assembly; touching our hearts in personal prayer; touching our hearts when we least expect it.

So I would like to suggest that two of the three outcomes worth your entertaining would be growth in this fear of the Lord and growth in this comfort of the Holy Spirit.

The fear of the Lord is the beginning of wisdom. It has to do with what develops in a child about his or her parents – Wow! Gee! It's that kind of attitude. It's a child-like thing and it usually grows best in sabbath. It grows best while sabbathing. It grows best when you're not trying to be in control; when you're not trying to be your own sovereign but when you're allowing the sovereignty of God to be seen and enjoyed and named and perceived.

The third possible outcome centers on our reason for being together. The outcome I would suggest is that my wealth, such as it is, begin to become transparent so that I begin to see God calling me in relation to its disposition; calling me through its disposition, its administration, even possibly its divestiture. The hoped-for outcome is that this commodity in my life begins to take on a transparency so that I am at ease in God about its deployment, its disposition, its allocation, its administration, its divestiture, whatever. An ease and a transparency is possible so that this commodity can stop being something profane, an obstacle, or full of ambiguity.

If you would accept a Roman Catholic theological language, money becomes a sacramental if I can see God calling me to use it in this way or that way. This to me is the primordial purpose of our weekend. That which postures as having its own power and capacity of "hauling me around" must begin to have a transparency. It can begin to be a sacramental, meaning a material object through which grace is able to come (God's graciousness to me and God's graciousness through me to others).

How does filthy lucre lose its filthiness? The ordinary way that we Christians have for something to be seen in terms of God is to take the measure of it in the light of the Word of God.

I like Psalm 1. I've always enjoyed the imagery. Blessed is the one who walks not counseled by the wicked, not in the way sinners walk, not as the insolent, sitting in the row with the scoffers. Blessed is the one who delights in the "torah" of the Lord, who is in the mind of the Lord, and who meditates on the Word day and night. Because she delights in knowing it, she spends time on the Word and finds things in the Word that she doesn't find in the newspapers or in conversation or from tapes or from books or from anywhere else. She finds them in the Word. What is that person like? That person is like a tree planted near streams; near running, living water that yields its fruit in due season and its leaf never withers because it's in touch with the Word.

The Word speaks to her. She is in touch with the Word. She gives time to the Word. She delights in the Word. There is a prospering in the life of such a one.

In contrast there are those like the chaff whom the wind blows away like tumbleweed because they're not in touch with the living Word. They're not in touch with the water.

If we want to achieve a transparency and pierce through the obscurity and ambiguity about wealth, the Word can be the carrier, the ramrod, the way in which transparency develops. There may be other ways, but that's the way which has been traditional for Judaism and Christianity through these many centuries.

I can be a person blown now this way, now that way, by this thought, by that thought, by this fear, by that fear, by this pressure, by that threat, by this guilt, by whatever! The Word is meant to speak to your heart about your unique relationship with the Lord and the disposition of your resources, given that relationship. That can't be done for you by me or by others. It can only be done by you. It can only be done by you if you give it time.

If you give it time and come to some degree of ability in listening to God's Word, there will be consolation, even delight. There is peace, wisdom, joy, and the comfort of the Holy Spirit. But if there is no fear of the Lord, if the Lord is taken for granted, or if "I've heard all this before." Where there is no fear of the Lord, no awe of the Lord, I don't find anything in the Word. I will remain unaddressed and empty.

I teach religious ethics at Chicago's Loyola University. We had an interesting experiment conducted a couple of weeks ago by the communications department at the university. The students' assignment was simply to have nothing to do from Friday evening until Monday morning with any media, like cassette, TV, radio, movie, newspaper, magazine, etc. They were to be on a total fast from the media. They were supposed to come in on Monday and describe the effects. Most of them had the same effects. I guess you'd call it withdrawal symptoms. They were going crazy. Even their relationships were going kaput! They couldn't stand being in that kind of quiet. It was astonishing to them. They didn't realize how much of their ordinary day is spent being bombarded by whatever – whatever they use to get bombarded. They were astonished that anyone could spend a weekend doing nothing without all the stuff that goes on before their eyes and into their ears for their whole lives.

The point is if you don't allow a little desert into this sabbath weekend, you won't know how thirsty you are. If you don't let in a little of the desert of sabbath, you won't realize how preempted your attention is by matters that keep you in your soul's topsoil. I think we have to go from being an information age to being an age that listens in depth in our hearts, to our hearts, in order to hear God. God speaks to hearts.

The first gift we have to offer each other this weekend is the gift of silence so that when you speak to one another you speak out of your depth. This would be the best gift we could give to one another. If you haven't plumbed your depths, don't just fill in the void with words. Let the other speak to you instead.

There's another Scripture with an image I'd like to mention here. It's from Matthew 7:21-27. "Not everyone that says to me Lord, 'Lord shall enter the Kingdom, but the one who does the will of My Father who is in heaven. On That Day (the Kingdom Day), many will say to me, 'Lord, did we not prophesy in Your name and cast out demons in Your name and do many mighty works in Your name?'" Weren't we very familiar with Your name? Didn't we throw Your name around a lot (out of seeming familiarity)? And then the Lord will say, "I never knew you."

"Everyone who hears these words of mine and does them will be counted among the wise who build their houses on rock. So that when the rains fall and the floods come and the winds blow and beat on that house, it will stand because it is founded on rock. And everyone who hears these words of mine and does not do them will be counted among the foolish who build their houses upon sand. So that when the rains fall and the floods come and the winds blow and beat against the house, it will fall and great will be the fall thereof."

So you get the picture. There is this great house. This is no small house. This house is amazingly furnished. This is a house with enormous adornment, but resting on what? It rests on the Word done after the Word is heard. It was interesting to me how many of you in your introductions of yourselves said something in effect that I can certainly identify with. In so many words you said, "I heard the Word before and then I went back into ambiguity or complacency or uncertainty or doubt."

A house built on rock is first of all a house in which the Word is heard and then the Word is done. It is in doing the Word heard that the house is built on rock. It is from not hearing the Word or upon hearing the Word not doing the Word that the sand stays at the foundation of the house, no matter how well adorned or great the house. It will fall.

Character is forged by doing the truth you know; by acting on the Word you hear; by being "single-minded" rather than ambiguous in yourself. These make for rock at the base.

So we have two images of two ways set before us in these readings. The first Psalm image is about either the chaff way or the "roots-touching-the-living-Word" way. In this reading from Matthew, the way is by the Word heard, Word done, rock forged – in contrast with Word not heard or heard and not done (maybe because you spend too much time in the house, on the house, for the house, mesmerized by the house) resulting in sand at the base and the whole thing passing away, once the winds come.

Now just a little reminder of the thing we've all heard in our churches for years. Remember what it is about the Word that is heard? The Word that comes from God is "living and active and sharper than any two-edged sword that pierces to the division of soul and spirit, of joints and marrow, and discerns the thoughts and intentions of the heart" (Hebrews 4:12-13).

What makes a strong foundation is a word heard and acted upon. What's the purpose of our weekend? It is to hear that word. How will we hear that word? Try to come to quiet in the silence. Do you know how much of our lives are spent arguing inside ourselves or with ourselves or arguing with somebody else or making sure we are up to date on the bad news and ignoring the Good News? Let it be a weekend of childlikeness so that I speak from that vulnerability and I speak from whatever depth I can attain to my brothers and sisters and hear my brothers and sisters from their depths.

Let me end with a prayer before we go into the silence this evening:

> Lord Jesus Christ, we name You Lord. For that is who You are. You are the Lord of life and You have given us life. You've given us life in You and You've given us life up to this moment in time. And we presume You'll give us life through this weekend. We want this to be a weekend in which we come to be delighted in You and find You delighted with us. We open ourselves to hear You speak to us whatever You would say. We really want to hear Your word. We really want our roots to touch the living water of Your Word. We really want to follow You more closely and not from afar looking over our shoulders and comparing ourselves to one another.
>
> We want to follow You up close. We want so much more of ourselves to love You. All of these things are impossible without Your taking action on us together and alone. So we ask You to please take this action – to speak to our hearts a word of knowledge so that our service of You can be of benefit to those closest to us and maybe even those far away from us. We ask You please, Lord Jesus, to act in power in our assembly. We thank You for the great, great privilege of serving You this weekend by simply listening to You speaking to our hearts. Glory be to the Father and to the Son and to the Holy Spirit, as it was in the beginning, is now, and ever shall be, world without end. Amen.

For Reflection

Sabbath has been a primary instrument used by God for the formation of Israel. Keeping holy the sabbath is a commandment that has never been abrogated. The Word could be savored deeply on sabbath. What place should sabbath have in my spiritual disciplines?

13

Transparency and Treasuring

This is holy ground. It's holy ground because the Lord is here, giving us a thirst for holiness. It's holy ground because the Lord is making us holy people. Today is sabbath and we attempt to keep holy the sabbath day. We will try to take what God has given us and make it malleable in God's hands. It is a holy day because we are God's own people called together and called singly to follow God's beloved Son. May You have Your way with us today, Lord. May this day be a day of praise to Your glory. May everything we cannot do ourselves and cannot even hope to do be done in us by You. We ask this through Jesus. Amen.

I have always understood Psalm 46:10 to be translated "Be still and know that I am God." But recently the exegetes have understood the Hebrew word *rapah* with a little more depth because of new linguistic data such as the Dead Sea Scrolls. Now they would translate "be still" as "let go." *"Let go and know that I am God."* This really fits into the tone of this sabbath weekend. Let go as a child lets go. A child doesn't even have to let go. A child just plays in the presence of its father and mother. A weekend of refreshment!

I have always liked what Abraham Joshua Heschel had to say about sabbath. He describes it as a cathedral built in time. So every seventh day you enter a cathedral built in time. And you are made holy if you "keep sabbath." It's a day for savoring versus studying. I suggested last night that we want to hear a word. And the best way to hear God's word is to *savor;* savoring is not an analytic act but a tasting that goes on with your heart.

The overall outcome I'd recommend for the reflections we have been doing (although your outcomes are your own business), is *transparency.* By worship and liturgy we seek to make the created things we have become offered things. Or as it is put in Latin, the *creata* (created things) become the *oblata* (offered things). Creata are made oblata if by our faith we make them available to God. So, just as the bread and wine (according to some denominations), while remaining bread and wine, become the bread of eternal life and the cup of eternal salvation because of God's action on those and because of our faith about God's action on those, so also the creata of our financial resources become the oblata by making them available to God. The creata of our financial resources can become the oblata and therefore a source of union with God and a source of spiritual growth rather than something that delays our union with God or proves an obstacle to such union. So the overall outcome I would recommend is transparency about your financial resources so that they become something that is malleable to God's purposes.

If "transparency" doesn't make it for you, how about "transfiguration" (transfigura refers to a passing over from one "figura" to the other). We're speaking of the transfiguration of both wealth as God sees it and even poverty as God sees it. A profound conversion is needed in each of our hearts so that I see my wealth or my poverty as God sees them.

Treasuring

It's the nature of the heart to treasure. The heart always migrates to the object that it treasures. My heart has many treasured objects. Your hearts have many treasured objects. Our hearts are always on the move toward those treasured objects. We treasure those objects in different degrees. Some of those treasured objects are preeminent and are meant to be preeminent. They bring an order to less treasured objects. Financial security is one of the treasured objects. And where it fits on the hierarchy of treasured objects will be the focus for this chapter.

Every treasured object triggers action on its behalf. Financial security is treasured or at least desired or sought after or deemed worthy of attention and concern. The trick to being thoroughly and fully Christian is to have *God* so treasured that the desire for financial security is subordinated to God. Of course I need financial security. That will always be the case. Materiality is endemic to our humanity. Though I will always need some financial security, the trick is to take that object of my affection and subordinate it to the treasure that is God.

Therefore, I must align my need for financial security with God. If I don't, I'll try to serve God *and* mammon (money that has become the object of trust). If I link my need for financial security to God, I can begin to surrender my financial security into God's hands and subordinate my "boodle" to God's purposes. These are really large and radical moves that only God can do in me. My will alone can't make those moves. But God can make those moves in me if I want them "to be done unto me."

This implies that I am willing to take my boodle out of its place of functioning as if it were a quasi-sovereign. Consequently, I don't maintain or administer it for itself or for myself. I maintain it and I administer it *for* God and *with* God because God is my preeminent treasure. If God is the treasured one, then the material treasure that I have inherited or that I have generated by my own efforts can become part of God's plan – subordinated to God's purposes, put in the hands of the mission that God is on.

Investment experts – people who have knowledge of investment – are very likely to add to the illusion of the sovereignty of my inheritance. Investment has all kinds of laws and when I put myself under the laws of investment, I'm almost certainly going to gain an increase of wealth. Investment information, fine. But determination solely by investment wizardry accords your boodle an autonomy it should not enjoy.

One of the ways Jesus used to motivate simple people (a lot simpler than ourselves) and poor people (a lot poorer than any of us) was to talk about how quickly a fortune can pass away. "Don't lay up for yourselves treasures on earth." Why? Because they have a transiency. They don't stay. They don't stay long. And they are never stable. There's the IRS, illness, hospital bills, unexpected disemployment, litigation, malpractice suits – the list is endless. In effect, the moth eats into them, the rust consumes them and thieves break in and steal. "Rather lay up for yourselves treasure in heaven where neither moth nor rust consume and where thieves do not break in and steal. For where your treasure is, there your heart will also be" (Luke 12:33-34).

A way of taking the measure of my wealth is to ask myself, "How can I make my financial resources part of Christ's purposes, part of Christ's mission, part of my way of following Christ, part of my way of being Christ's disciple, thus removing them from any autonomy or ambivalence and or strutting they might seem to do as if they're a source of my power and well being." How do I take the profanity out of my financial resources and make them sacred, thus giving them permanence?

Recall again the story about the rich farmer with all the grain in Luke's Gospel. (Luke is the one most involved with our question, as you know.) The story is in Luke 12:15ff. It all begins with a man coming up to Jesus and speaking of a dispute he is having with his brother about their inheritance. Jesus says to take heed and beware of all forms of greed (pleonexia). That is, beware of all desire for *more* of what you have, for your life does not consist in your possessions. Instead, seek to become rich in the sight of God, is Jesus' exhortation.

If we cannot come to a transparency in our perception of and use of our financial resources then the advice gets more drastic. "Fear not, little flock, for it is your Father's good pleasure to give you the Kingdom." Do you want it? Do you want God's reign over you to be all-important? It all depends on whether you want this. It's the Father's good pleasure to give you the Kingdom. And if you don't know your reaction to the offer, then let His next words sink in: "Sell your possessions and give alms and provide yourselves with purses that do not grow old with a treasure in the heavens that does not fail where no thief approaches and no moth destroys. For where your treasure is there your heart will also be" (Luke 12:33-34).

Notice what the options are. Your boodle cannot *stay* neutral. Either it becomes malleable in God's hands or it has to be divested. These are the only options. Trying to keep the boodle neutral makes for a split consciousness. It makes you *two* people. It makes for somebody who is a person with two objects of trust – a person of faith and of disbelief and a person of trust and of distrust. And in that battle mammon will win! That's Jesus' contention. "No servant can serve two masters. Either he will hate the one and love the other, or he will be devoted to the one and despise the other. You cannot serve both God and money" (Luke 16:13). In this split mammon wins because it has an immediacy to it. It has a tangibility to it. This is one of the deepest battles in the soul.

Inheritance

Some of these themes I've already spoken about in terms of treasure I will comment on in relation to inheritance.

You have said things about your inheritances. One of you was advised by his therapist to try to have fun with your inheritance. And that became an aspiration for you. That's a good aspiration. Another of you described your inheritance as something of a curse – especially a negative factor in how your relationships play out over against your inheritance. A number of you talked about ambiguity and ambivalence in relation to your inheritance. One of you used the word *paranoia* in relation to your inheritance. Several of you complained about yourselves as having lapsed into a religious complacency because of your inheritance.

The primary theme that laces together the Old and New Testaments is the theme of *covenant*. Covenant is God's embrace of those with whom God covenants. The embrace is close and intimate with those who allow God to embrace them. The embrace is remote for those who keep God at a distance.

One subset to the theme of covenant is the theme of *inheritance*. Within the panorama of covenant or embrace is the theme of inheritance. Abraham is promised an inheritance. Moses leads the people to the beginnings of receiving their inheritance in the land of Canaan where there takes place the apportionment of lands to each of the tribes and in turn to each of the families. So inheritance begins to become tangible as we go in time from the patriarchs through Moses into Israel. The inheritance begins to become tangible, and the first tangibility of the inheritance is the land. "You haven't hewn out cisterns and you haven't cultivated these lands and you haven't planted these trees and yet I say they are yours" (Deuteronomy 6:11).

They're yours to use, but it's My land. You're to cultivate this land and enjoy this land with a spirit of thanksgiving and an awareness that this land is not wholly yours. It is given to you by Me. You are to cultivate the land according to My mind. You'll find My mind expressing itself in and through Torah. Hold the land and cultivate the land and give thanks for the land that I have given to you.

The land in Israel was God's down payment, or first installment, on an inheritance that was to be eternal (a new heavens and a new earth) in which God would be all in all.

We come to the New Testament and find that the Son is the sole heir (Mark 12:7). But all who are in the Son are joint heirs with the Son (Romans 8:17). And the first installment on the inheritance according to the New Testament is the gift of the Holy Spirit (Romans 8:23). So what *land* was for Israel, *Spirit gift* is for the new people of Israel.

What is the function of the Spirit gift – this down payment on the inheritance, or first installment of the inheritance? Among several, one function of the Spirit gift that stands out is to speak truth to the heart – the truth about who God is, the truth about who I am, the truth about where these things come from that we have, the truth about how to use these things as stewards of God's resources.

"If you are led by the Spirit of God you are children of God" (Romans 8:14). The purpose of this Spirit gift is to be led into truth – into all truth about the things you have to know in order to come into your final inheritance; into your full inheritance; into your eternal inheritance – and to know how to use the resources of time in order to attain that final inheritance. "When we cry Abba, Father, it is the Spirit bearing witness with our spirit about the truth of ourselves, that we are children of God. And if we're children then we're heirs of God and fellow heirs with Christ. . ." (Romans 8:16ff.). So being children of God inevitably means being followers of Christ and joint heirs with Christ of the inheritance that He has won for us. Our earthly treasure must be evaluated in terms of our eternal inheritance, our permanent inheritance that Christ has won for us – the inheritance that the Spirit is given to teach us about.

I must inquire into the effect (and each of us will find different answers) that my present treasure has on this permanent inheritance that I've been promised. Is my *present* treasure making my *eternal* inheritance less important or irrelevant or unnecessary? Or is the way in which I dispose of my present treasure only adding to my desire for this full inheritance that God intends to bestow on me? Is my heavenly inheritance of such worth to me that I would forfeit my present inheritance if so asked? If it began to be a substitute for or proved to be an obstacle to that heavenly treasure, that treasured union with God, what would I do with it so that it ceased to be so?

That's a tough word. And it goes back to Luke 12. "Fear not, little flock, for it is your Father's good pleasure to give you the Kingdom." There are many synonyms for our heavenly inheritance. Grace is one. Glory is another. Resurrection of the body is another. The Kingdom is the best, I think.

"Fear not, little flock, for it is your Father's good pleasure to give you the Kingdom." Either make disposition of your present inheritance in the light of this promise *or* "sell your possessions and give alms and provide yourselves with purses that do not grow old with a treasure in the heavens that does not fail, where no thief approaches nor moth destroys. Where your treasure is, there your heart will also be." That's why I say there is no such thing as a neutral treasure or inheritance. It moves you one way or it moves you the other. It can't stay neutral very long.

For most of you, as far as I can understand, it's not likely that you will be asked to divest totally of your treasure. For most of you it will be a matter of discerning by means of the Spirit gift the best way to deepen your relationship with God through the ongoing disposition of your earthly treasure.

Question and Answer Time

Participant: When I think I've got the answer, that's when it seems I'm on a banana peel. So there's this element of not knowing and of ambiguity that has always seemed to me as far as I ever got. (This participant seemed in favor of keeping money issues open by citing permanent ambiguity and uncertainty.)

John Haughey: I can't disagree with your experience, but I just wouldn't make keeping all your options open a goal! Some people would rather be in the hunt than come to the catch. That doesn't deny that ambiguity suffuses much of life. I'm just suggesting that the goal of the quest is possession of the truth. In other words the *telos* (the end point) of the quest is to come to truth. Some

people make an ideology out of always keeping everything open.

Same Participant: But don't we live in the already and the
not yet?

John Haughey: Sure. But the already is the already received Spirit. And the Spirit's function is to teach. And
the Spirit's yield is truth. And truth calls for action. An
action taken on the basis of truth understood yields more
truth!

Of course, it's always a journey, but eventually we
arrive. I used the philosophical term teleology before.
You may prefer the theological word – the eschatology.
In either case, you can't make eschatology only a journey
motif. There's the already and the not yet. But you can't
use the not yet as an excuse to not begin to experience
in time the eternal inheritance that has been given to us.
This inheritance is given to us now in part in and
through the Spirit and is meant to teach us about the
disposition of what we possess now. That present understanding of the disposition of things now – our present
treasure – has to have some degree of closure to it. We
have to make choices. That's my point. If we leave everything open, then leaving everything open means we
never really come to fulness. You act on faith! And you
act in faith. And you act now on the basis of what you
have come to see and understand.

There is an assurance the Spirit can give, a "blessed
assurance." It's not absolute; it always has to undergo testing. You're always in need of testing the Spirit. But there
is an assurance. It's never absolute, but there's enough
light to say, This direction seems right. This other direction seems wrong.

Participant: There is hope for me in what you said. If we take action based on the truth we know now, it will lead to further truth. In my life I've made some pretty dumb actions, but they've led me to some further truth that I don't think I would have learned if I hadn't taken what in hindsight seems like a dumb step but was the best I knew to do at the time.

John Haughey: That's why this thing about affections or evoking action from what is treasured is so important for me. You can *know* whether your heart wants the Kingdom or whether it doesn't. You can know whether the world is so much with you that the promised inheritance becomes unimportant. You know that. Your heart knows that. You're sure that your heart does or doesn't want this or that. There's not a lot of ambiguity if you are in touch with your heart.

That's why I started this session off with treasure and treasuring. The heart always migrates to objects of affection. And every one of us is capable of reflection on "Where does my heart migrate to?" "What is the hierarchy of my treasures?" "Is my boodle tucked into and under the treasure that is Christ, or is it independent of the treasure that is Christ?" That's the key! And your heart will tell you.

Participant: That's where the silence comes in. When the silence goes, then what I treasure really becomes confused.

John Haughey: Yes! Chances are good that without the silence my actions are propelled by my disordered appetites. *With* the silence my actions are propelled by my heart.

Participant: Would you unpack that word *mammon* a little bit?

John Haughey: Mammon is boodle that creates its own law. In other words, it is its own sovereign. . . . It is money become "sleazy"! The Aramaic root of mammon is "that in which I put my trust." It becomes an object of trust. But you can't have the two objects of trust, God and mammon. The financial resources become their own law when they become trusted. The message of the Gospels is you can't have two sovereigns running your life. Transparency, therefore, becomes an issue. If your financial resources begin to be seen the way God sees them and begin to be used in terms of your understanding of God as the Spirit teaches you that, then you haven't allowed financial resources to become mammonized.

Another way of saying things here: Everybody has financial resources. Some have very little. There's a study that came out this week from the IMF or World Bank that said there are more than 1 billion people in this world today living on less than one dollar per day. That is stunning! But all of us have to have material resources, financial resources in order to express ourselves in our humanity. We have to eat, drink, and clothe ourselves. Now those material or financial resources, whether a lot or a little, can be their own law or they can be used as coming from God and leading to God. When they are their own law, they are mammon. When they are taken as coming from God and leading to God, they have been demammonized.

It is a spiritual issue. The problem is not the money. The problem is not in the financial resources. They are neutral. But our use of it does not stay neutral. That's why I say there is no such thing as a neutral boodle!

There is nothing wrong with enormous wealth per se. Recall Jesus' handling of two wealthy people. Zacchaeus was a wealthy person and was described as such. Jesus did not call for divestment. He asked for an invitation to dinner! The result was divestment of part of what he owned. The rich young ruler comes up to Him and Jesus calls for divestment. Now why did Jesus act differently with those two wealthy people? He acted differently because presumably He saw in the case of Zacchaeus that Zacchaeus did not think he *was* what he *had*. In the case of the rich young man He sensed a problem – that the man was so identified with what he had that he couldn't divest himself from it. He handled him differently. That's why I said that I had no idea what word you are going to hear. All I know is that it is going to be a word tailored to your situation and to what you have become in relation to your resources. These things have to be dealt with by the Lord person by person, heart by heart – each heart open to Christ.

Test the attractions and the repugnances you feel in relation to what you are hearing because it's very likely that the Spirit will speak to us through attractions and repugnances much more clearly than through ideas! That's how the Spirit usually speaks.

It's usually through the use of spiritual disciplines that you come to transparency. One spiritual discipline that comes from my own Ignatian Jesuit tradition is the discipline of going through a reflective action on "Why is that repugnant?" "Why is that attractive?" Ignatius taught what he called the prayer of examen. Whether done twice a day or twice a year is not the point. The point is I go back over the history of my *affectivity* in the period of the morning or the afternoon or the day and see the heart's leaps and the heart's depressions. So I check the remembered heart moves and I review those. Why did that leave me "up"? Why did that leave me "down"? By this hindsight prayer I frequently find a different perception of how God was speaking to me than I had in the course of just moving through the day.

Participant: This Examen prayer sounds like the same kind of process I undertake when I journal. Isn't it intending the same effect as journaling?

John Haughey: It is a good observation, except that I believe journaling's intent is more a psychological sorting out, whereas the explicit purpose of the Examen is prayer and light to see the reviewed past in God's presence, with God's help so that I might get a graced glimpse at how it looks upon reflection. But this distinction presumes I know what the journaler has in mind and I'm sure this will vary person to person.

For Reflection

The grace this section seeks is to be able to achieve a transparency with respect to our financial resources so that we can see them in terms of God and serve God through their use. Otherwise an opacity about them develops and dealing with them as separate deepens a split consciousness. Inheritance, too, must come to be seen in the same way.

14

Love of Self and Wealth

I came to an understanding about the person of Jesus during Holy Week that I think is germane to the subject we're wrestling with. If we try to know anything about God, obviously the best place to go is to God's incarnate Son. If we want to know the mind of God about anything, the best place to go is to the Son of God. If we want to know what kind of person God would like us to be, follow and replicate the Son.

It had been my practice during Holy Week to try to keep Thursday, Friday, and Saturday unencumbered as a time for reflection. I had always seen Jesus during the events of His passion, death, and resurrection as either loving God the Father or loving His disciples or loving us. This past Holy Week I saw it differently. I want to tell you what the difference was because I think it clarifies what we've been trying to do in our theological reflection on wealth.

I don't know that I could prove it, but my hypothesis is that what sets Jesus apart experientially from the rest of us is the amount of love of Himself that He had. I don't know that a man could have undergone what He had to undergo if He didn't love Himself more than I love myself or you love yourself and all of us have ever been trained or invited to love ourselves.

We have a wonderful theologian in the Catholic Church, Karl Rahner. One of his great essays is on the indivisibility of the love of God and love of neighbor. Basically the idea is that there is only one love. The love that we have for neighbor comes from God and leads to God, and the love we have for God comes to neighbor and unites us to neighbor and leads us back to God.

What I felt very attracted to this past Holy Week was to add to Rahner's analysis the third object of love – the self. "Love the Lord your God with you whole heart, your whole soul, your whole mind and your whole strength and your neighbor as *yourself*" (Luke 10:27). It's that third object of love – the self – that I think is the unnoticed "sleeper" in explaining Jesus. It's the absence of that love of self, I think, that is the reason why we are not each centers of love – irradiating love from ourselves to others and to God. If you cut off one of the three objects of love, you abort the mission!

So to go back to Rahner's point – yes love is indivisible, but there also has to be love of self. In proportion to the love of self there can be love of neighbor and in turn love of God. So I beheld this Man going to His death with this odd (for me) kind of contemplation: This Man loved Himself!

I watched this self-love in the person of Jesus, and these were some of the thoughts I had about it: It wasn't self-induced. It wasn't self-generated. It was *received*. It gets overheard by us at two points in His ministry – at His baptism and at His transfiguration. "You are My beloved Son"; "This is My beloved Son. . ." He took in the fact of His belovedness. He accepted it. He received it. It would have been a most profound kind of disobedience for Him to say, "That's not true."

Twentieth-century Christologies tend to be what are called ascending Christologies rather than descending. An ascending Christology tries to see the human consciousness of Jesus develop the way the human consciousness of anybody develops. So if you take this question of how Jesus let this message of being beloved into His human consciousness, I think you'd have to see His mother as playing a part in that. She seemed to be able to take being singled out as "blessed among women" without recoiling in self-reproach and without saying, "No, you couldn't mean me."

Mary seemed capable of pondering in her heart the word that was spoken to her and the words that were spoken around her. She made room in her heart and therefore would have taught Jesus to make room in His heart for words spoken to him. I invite you to see that the power of Jesus' ministry was in proportion to His ability to let in, to take in, to receive, and to own this description of Himself as beloved!

By contrast, those whom He called to be with Him were limited because of some kind of inability to accept themselves. How do we know that? Because the disciples closest to Jesus were always trying to outmaneuver one another; to get to the first place (e.g., Luke 22:24). Their insecurity is the telltale sign of their inability to be rooted in a received self-love. Whatever the source of their self-reproach, which must have bordered sometimes on self-loathing or self-contempt, it made it very difficult for them to love one another. And if they remained in that condition, it was very unlikely that Jesus' final and primordial commandment, to love one another, would be kept well by them.

You're never going to have a community of people who love one another if the individuals in that community do not know and accept themselves as loved. So I meditated on Jesus washing the feet of His followers of the "grime of decades" in which they were taught by their parents, leaders, teachers, and mentors that they had to *perform* themselves into self-worth. They had to *merit* self-valuing and self-acceptance by ongoing performance.

That's at least what they were taught by the blind guides who had a performance criterion of self-acceptance.

I reflected on the fact that Jesus kept on – notwithstanding the fact of rejection from almost every side. He did not surrender that inner core of certainty of being loved. His self-worth was not contingent on people's acceptance of Him.

There seem to be *two* different kinds of indivisibilities. There is the indivisibility of love of self, God, and neighbor. And there is another indivisibility, which is deadly for our societies, for our neighborhoods, for our communities. That is the indivisibility of self-contempt, neighbor indifference (maybe even neighbor contempt), and God indifference (maybe even God contempt).

Granted, there are two kinds of self-love – one praiseworthy and one reprehensible. The reprehensible kind of self-love is a love of self based on performance or delusion or narcissistic or unwarranted dreams of grandeur. The other kind of self-love, the one I see in Jesus, is the one that receives the word spoken to oneself – a word of love.

This then turned for me into a reflection on what Eucharist was at the last supper and what Eucharist is, at least in my own devotional life and maybe in some of yours.

Eucharist is a time in which belovedness – the statement and the fact – is received. It is a time at which one becomes a special object of Christ's own love and is invited to take in that love as it is mediated through the symbols of bread and wine. Of course, one can find a false source of self-love. That is, I think, where Jesus' statements about wealth come in.

Why did He say to beware of riches? Why did He say it is harder for a camel to pass through the eye of a needle than for a rich man to enter the Kingdom of God?

This wasn't a cheap exhortation to not be greedy. His hearers knew what greed was, and they didn't need Him to exhort them to not be greedy.

What specifically is the problem with wealth in relation to this whole matter of self-love? That's what I'd like you to examine. The problem with wealth is not so much with greed or selfishness. It is more foundational than that. Jesus saw that riches were an accessible and a seductive place on which to base one's self-worth. I think that was the core of it – to take the measure of my worth in terms of my wealth! When my wealth is my worth, then my worth is rooted in a fallacy, in a falsehood. When what I have tells me of my worth, I'm in trouble because the "have" keeps shifting.

If one doesn't love the self that God loves and that God has made and that God is calling forth, then one looks for a pseudo-self to love. And the person of wealth has a pseudo-self very accessible to him or her. One immediately moves toward accumulation in order to grow in self-worth. And any diminution of what I have threatens to result in a reduction of self-worth.

When the basis of self-worth is something as superficial as wealth, then relationships with other people become flawed. The depth of mutuality that is possible for a person in a relationship in which self-worth is located at the superficial level of "have" is going to leave such a person shallow and lonely all his or her life because deep can never call to deep.

If we are not in touch with our true self, then the true self is never on the line in moments of potential mutuality. If you see yourself and your worth in terms of what you have or in terms of performance, you will see others' worth in terms of what they have or their performance. What a lonely place to be!

Equally problematic will be our relationship to God. Our relationship to God is deeply and negatively impacted by a mediated source of security that isn't built on the rock of our own lovability as received.

This brings us to the subject of idolatry. If the basis for self-worth is wealth in some form, either wealth as such or what wealth can procure (addictions easily accrue to wealth), then an idol (though never so named) becomes the perceived, acted-upon source of my well-being. I don't have to relate to God with the dependency of a childlike need because this (intermediary, unnamed as such) idol is functioning fairly well in meeting my needs. I can remain a believer, but I relate to God infrequently and always superficially because I don't in fact regularly need God.

What is an idol? It is a treasured object that I load up with expectations it cannot deliver. I give it a power to promise well-being, which it cannot deliver. It becomes a center of attention and devotion. It always leaves me wanting for more of what it promises.

Idolatry in the Hebrew Scriptures is always looked on as a betrayal of a relationship that is meant to be exclusive. Relationship with God is usually put in marital terms, as in Hosea 2, Jeremiah 2, Ezekiel 16. Yahweh comes across as a jealous lover who wants me to say yes to the love that's being given me and to accept that love.

There's a ferocity in the jealousy of Yahweh because Yahweh cannot be indifferent to my response. If He was, He wouldn't keep coming after me trying to name me in terms of His love of me.

Why am I unable to receive the name "beloved"? The relationship between this inability and wealth is critical to know because if God's love for me is the basis of my self-acceptance, then there will be a freedom to make use of what I have as a way of responding in love to God.

If I don't let in this love of God for me, then the wealth I have too easily functions at the foundational level of self-understanding as my deepest worth. And that's the tragedy of wealth and why Jesus said to beware of it! Beware of it, for it is very subtle and it is extremely seductive.

Let me sum up what I'm saying here: There's a morally neutral character about wealth that ceases to be morally neutral as soon as I use it to name myself falsely. The ability to hear that God loves and loves me is then diminished, maybe even eradicated.

If what I have, own, desire, consume begins to substitute for a true self-acceptance and a true self-love then my house is built on sand.

I see Jesus as the person who let in being called "beloved," which is meant for us as well. He let it in. He received it. And I think all His powerful loving God and neighbor – all the way to the point of self-emptying – follows from that self-acceptance. When we have another basis of self-acceptance than God's unconditional love, then we're probably close to the spiritual condition of idolatry as it functioned in the Old Testament. Idolatry was the betrayal of a marital union.

You can use a lot of different things to misread or miss altogether God's love of you, but Jesus had a particular concern about wealth, which is why He kept bringing it up. Apparently He thought it had a greater ability to seduce and substitute for the self-acceptance that was the basis for the commandment to love God, neighbor, and self.

Participant: Where did you get this insight into Jesus? It is close to what Henri Nouwen says in his book *Life of the Beloved.*

John Haughey: I haven't read Nouwen. I suspect it is from a book I wrote in 1971 called *The Conspiracy of God.* There I got interested in Jesus' gradual process of naming Himself. First He named Himself as special. Then He named Himself as beloved. Then He named Himself in special Son terms. Then He named Himself Kurios, "Lord," and various other things. But the teacher in this whole process for Jesus was the Holy Spirit. And that's why the book was called *The Conspiracy of God: The Holy Spirit and Us.* I think that's where this theme of beloved started in me.

Probably Jesus didn't spend as much time on receiving His belovedness as he did on the One who was speaking love to Him. Once your eye is on the One speaking love to you, which is God calling you beloved in the beloved, then you're called even beyond that warmth in a direction where you lose the self and find the self in love. The call of Christ is to abide in His love. But then you have to love those whom God loves. And to love those whom God loves is the way we both lose and gain our life.

So now let's go to the microphones for your extension or correction of the themes that were proposed this weekend – or for clarification if that's necessary.

Participant: Almost a digression I guess, but yesterday you were talking about the Jesuit martyrs in El Salvador and you talked about the difference between theology and doctrine. For some reason it troubled me because it seems to me that we're almost called to live more in the theological realm than in the doctrinal realm because by the time it gets to be doctrine it's institutionalized and probably ought to be forgotten anyway. That's a harsh statement, John, but that was my immediate reaction.

John Haughey: Let me pick apart a couple of the things you said. I wouldn't want to make isomorphic the doctrinal and the institutional. Then it would seem like the Holy Spirit who tells truth to the churches, which is what the Spirit does, ends up a loser in the institution. We can't afford that kind of disdain for the institution. The institutionalization of Christianity is where incarnation had to go. The Word was made flesh. The Word is continually made flesh. Flesh has to take on structure, become institutional.

And we can't afford to have a disdain for the fact of institution because we make the institutions that we work and live in. The institutions are simply the embodiment of the sum total of our acting selves. The fault is us and ours and in us, not in the institutions as such. The 1960s had a lot of disdain for institutions, including ecclesial institutions, and I think we can do better than that. The Word has to be made flesh and flesh always has to be institutional.

Participant: John, I could use some help with the order of things. I feel that if it were a book, you started us off on chapter 3 (the transparency of wealth and earthly goods), and we ended up last night with chapter 1. Now I'd like you to give a paragraph of introduction to that book with chapter 1 (about my belovedness) coming first.

John Haughey: Let me tell you why I proceeded in that order. I think it takes a whole day for us to get to the deeper issues. And although I don't think that means we have to play around for a whole day, the focus that we had in coming here had to do with wealth. So I started with what I thought people expected but ended up with where I thought people ought to start. So if I were to put this thing in a book, I'd start with last night. If I put it in the order of expectation, I'd start where I started.

And about the entitlement of my book, *The Holy Use of Money:* I wanted to call it *The Transubstantiation of Wealth.* But who's going to know what "transubstantiation" means except someone who is 50 years old and Roman Catholic, which limits the possibility of marketing the book?

Transubstantiation is still a term that appeals to me – to make the substance of one thing substantially another thing. To transpose the substantial character of it while allowing it to stay the same. As with the bread and wine, so also the money stays the same.

Participant: How do you interface transubstantiation with incarnation? Is there a progression here?

John Haughey: Let me try it this way. When Word is spoken into flesh, flesh is transformed. The word *beloved* was spoken into the flesh of Jesus and He was transformed. This of course was after the incarnation. And He gradually over time began to receive the full word of who He was, which had the tag "belovedness" at the core. Then it was for Him as it was for those who follow Him to pronounce a word into the flesh that they are surrounded by – the material reality that they are surrounded by. And when we name; when we pronounce the word that we want to pronounce on our wealth – a word that comes to us through faith and in faith enlightened by the Holy Spirit – then that material reality is transubstantiated.

So you go from the Word made flesh to the word that the Word made flesh pronounces on reality. What starts off incarnation ends up transfiguration or transubstantiation or icon or transparency or alignment or correlation. We used five different ways of trying to get wealth to be a means to valued ends – to ends valued in faith. The way we do that is to name the reality of those things rather than have those things name our reality.

Adam started off naming the animals. But soon the animals were naming Adam. It is a perversion when money speaks to us and we are not speaking to it. There is a new transformation needed. Our culture makes it difficult for the proclamation of truth about our money to take root. An alternative community culture is a point still needed to name together the realities around us.

Participant: I was interested in your comments about family. Might you be saying that in making the family a kind of idol and putting too much stock in it or putting too much energy into it, that in some way we lose the transparency that both the family and money should have?

John Haughey: Yes. Every family that gets too close becomes a source of disappointment. That's the experience that we all have, isn't it? That's the experience of idolatry too. If you invest something finite with infinity, you're always going to be dashed. Those of you who have wealth would probably testify to this readily. Part of the denial wealth induces is to keep it private, keep it "among us." Keep it "in house." Keep it to ourselves. We're the only ones who understand. They (out there) don't understand. And the more it is kept at home, the less healthy the members become. Now that's not a statement about any one wealthy family. It is a "read" of people like John Levy and others who have written about great wealth. It's an extremely dangerous commodity to domesticate.

One of the themes that came up last year was how best do you love your children in relationship to inheritance? That was a cause of extreme conflict in the group that was here last year. Very few people felt they had come to any clear resolution about it.

Participant: I wanted to go back to yesterday afternoon when you were talking about justice giving. You commented that divestiture could be too convenient a way to dispose of one's boodle. I wanted to share some of our experience of going through divestiture as being a tremendous experience of justice giving and empowerment for us. We came to see that we had a certain quantity of potential empowerment that could be utilized.

It became a question of control for us, whether we chose to control the money or put it into the hands of folks who'd be able to utilize it for social change. So in going through this divestiture process, we had this tremendous empowerment happen for people who had talent and vision but who lacked capital. They were able to do things that we never would have been able to do by keeping control ourselves. It was a really exciting process, and we felt empowered ourselves too as we went through it. So I'd like to hold this out as another possibility in relation to justice giving.

John Haughey: Let me say this about what you're saying. If I unpackage what I meant by what might have seemed to be a dismissal of divestiture in relation to justice, what I was thinking about there were people who for whatever reason, either a lack of sophistication or from guilt or impatience or a sense of need to be clean or whatever the motivation – simply remove themselves from their inheritance or they give their inheritance away. I like your bringing me back to a nuance of my statement. Your form of divestment was good. Also it was better when it comes to justice because you thought through with other people how others could be empowered by the power that was latent in your wealth. Wealth is congealed energy.

You ended up with what could be called divestment or divestiture. You lost what you had but empowered many, including yourselves, by what you did. Justice giving may well have as its bottom line divestment, but the best justice giving is that which thinks structurally about how empowerment goes on.

It is just beautiful to me that the impetus for your divestiture came from your identification with people. The function of wealth is solidarity. And what you're describing was that you had the experience of solidarity, then wealth came to you, and you reduced the wealth in order to retain the solidarity.

Justice giving involves creation of solidarity. Almsgiving may be no less loving but it is unilateral. And it doesn't necessarily imply solidarity. That's why justice giving is such a critical issue. I wouldn't want to say one is better and one is worse. But it's extremely important for us to think in structural terms – structural terms meaning the consequences are solidarity.

Participant: Unless we follow Christ first, we will not challenge our family tradition and history when it comes to our inheritance. Both the woman challenging her spouse and any of us challenging our family history with inheritance know the risk and the cost. But I think that's how demanding Christ is. "Unless you hate your father, mother, brother, sister, or wife you cannot follow me."

John Haughey: My first comment is *Amen!* My second comment is that it seems to me that a lot of the ideals that we have been exhorted to live by, which are valid ideals and do come from the Gospel, if they don't have self-acceptance as a base, end up debasing the people who are trying to live them because they circumvent this first act of accepting oneself as loved. So the person who cannot accept herself as loved could expend the whole psychic and spiritual energy of her life trying to be servant of others. And you know people like that who exhaust themselves at the level of superego. In other words, this is the way I ought to be and until I can perform at the level of the ought, then there is self-disparagement – all very subtle.

So that's my comment on trying to become a servant and circumventing the call to receive being loved. There is a profound perversion when Christianity is one long falling short of the mark of perfection without ever loving yourself. And then if you become a preacher in one form or another (and everyone is officially or unofficially), then you keep putting the same cart-before-the-horse trip on everybody else! So it's only a person who can be self-determining, it seems to me, who can afford to surrender self-determination and be healthy.

Same Participant: Henri Nouwen says that you can only give up your life if you have one.

Participant: Being beloved is not necessarily a warm and comforting feeling. It's a love that is leading us to places that we wouldn't choose to go. And to love ourselves is to challenge ourselves to look at going to places that we wouldn't necessarily choose to go.

Appendix

"Vienna Diary: Moving from Wrongs to Rights," by John Haughey, S.J. Reprinted with permission of *Woodstock Report* 35 (October 1993). I have inserted this appendix to fill out the ideas about "Justice Giving" that were elaborated in Chapter 7, which has the same title. People of wealth usually have causes with which they identify. When those causes promote human rights, they deserve to be singled out for acclaim.

The U.N. sponsored Conference on Human Rights is due to get going tomorrow. This beautiful city is filled with delegates from more than 160 countries and rights activists from more than 1000 nongovernmental organizations. The conference participants I have spoken with are full of either great hopes or great fears. The hopers are full of passion about their respective causes. The more sanguine are those delegates who are aware that on three separate occasions this year, representatives have tried to put together a working document and have failed miserably. Rights are a source of considerable discomfort to regimes which do not want a portion of their population having recourse to a moral authority and measure beyond their states which can be used to critique their practices and policies. This is the great value of human rights.

I have decided to do a diary of this conference rather than a conference report because it gives me more leeway to be impacted by people and special moments instead of having to cover everything. In that spirit let me begin by indicating today is Corpus Christi, the feast of the Body and Blood of Christ. In thinking about this liturgy I have come to realize that my angle of vision on rights is very much influenced by my vision of eucharist. The line in today's readings brought this home to me: "This bread is my flesh for the life of the world" (John 6:53). Both eucharist and rights make life in this world possible. Both are God initiated while humanly received. Both invite a response in the form of actions that gather rather than scatter. Although only a portion of the world's population receive the bread that is his "flesh for the life of the world," every human being is scripted by God with a dignity which is insured by God-given rights. The "life of the world" will only be as good as the world's citizens' knowledge of and respect for one another's rights.

June 14

One of the curiosities I have had about this conference is whether the participants mean roughly the same thing when they speak of human rights. I read enough about the initial Declaration of Human Rights that was forged by the U.N. in 1948 to know that it was thin on theory and that the foundation of the cited rights was not articulated and could not bear too close a scrutiny. To my great surprise, rather than disaggregating the several sets of rights and subjecting each of them to a greater scrutiny, one of this conference's purposes is to win an agreement by aggregating them and seeing them as indivisible.

Getting conferees and nations to agree on the "indivisibility" of rights in this first UN conference on human rights to be held in 25 years will take some doing because, while western nations are clear that the rights they respect and want respected are political and civil, many other nations want social and economic rights given primacy. The first set of rights insures the self-determination of persons and peoples. The second insures the material well being of persons and people. Accepting their indivisibility will mean that both sets of rights will be respected and taken to be primary, human rights.

The speech I was most interested in hearing this first day was that of Secretary of State, Warren Christopher, because our country has not believed in the indivisibility of rights. We have let peoples' material well being be a matter that relies on the market, their own enterprise and initiative, or charity and social programs if citizens can't provide for their own material well being. For these reasons, the U.S. has never ratified the U.N. Covenant on Economic, Social and Cultural Rights. Sure enough, Christopher directly addressed this weakness by indicating that the Clinton Administration will seek to get the Senate to ratify that important ESCR Covenant. Without such an effort the adamant stance of the United States at this conference for countries to ratify and act on the other Covenant which deals with Civil and Political Rights would rightly be read as self-serving and hypocritical.

Two other points made by the main speakers this first day are worthy of mention. The Secretary-General of the U.N., Boutros Boutros-Ghali, stressed the need to make human rights the "ultimate norm of politics." How revolutionary that would be! He showed he was aware that rights are manipulated by cynical governments who use them as a cloak to cover their self-interested realpolitik. Further, he warned the delegates that history condemned sovereignties that functioned in ruthless despite of their own citizens' rights. Finally, this beleaguered

U.N. leader advised the conference not to seek to "define new rights" but "to persuade states to adopt existing instruments and apply them effectively."

The elected president of the conference, Alois Mock, Austria's Minister of Foreign Affairs, explained the venturesome goal of the gathering: to craft a human rights agenda for the 21st century. He also explained that since human rights are common to all, they are not bestowed on the individual by the state but are "part of man's very nature." That was a welcome position to hear articulated since it put the conference on notice that something as universal and particular as individual human nature was the locus germane to rights analyses. The balking nations here have complained that rights are a Western concept and that cultures, traditions, and religions that were not in on the early United Nations conversations that led to the 1948 Declaration find the idea of rights alien to them. The rights groups from these balking countries deny this. The Dali Lama, for example, concurs that "the majority of Asian people do not support the view" that rights are alien to their cultures.

Today was a good start; the mood was upbeat. I suspect a number of those attending in one capacity or another felt like world citizens, maybe for the first time. I know I did.

June 15

The very rich conversations here on rights which are going on all over the place have triggered my imagining a world without rights and realized how Hobbesian a world it would be, with life brutish, nasty, and short for all of us. The theologian in me is begining to realize that the divine agenda and the human agenda conjoin at the point of the promotion of human well being through human rights. "Gloria Dei, vivens homo." God's glory is the human person, every person, fully flourishing.

Take socio-economic rights, for example. When observed they assure a degree of material well being which, if disregarded, one has to grovel, animal-like, for food, water, shelter. But such basic rights mirror the divine agenda for humans. The divine agenda for living things can be observed in the abundance supplied by creation. But do not the fish of the sea and the birds of the air fare better living off of the goods of the earth than the majority of humans? In a world population of just over 5 billion humans, 1 billion live in absolute poverty, another billion on the margin of poverty and daily 35,000 children die of hunger and disease. Although rights are gradually becoming part of the human agenda, their observance is abysmal; their violation screams out from these three facts alone but the 1000 booths in the NGO floor of this conference makes the degrees and kinds of violation alarmingly tangible. Who are the violators?

All on whom rights claims are made who have the wherewithal to respond to some degree and don't. Insofar as I can and don't, I am one of the violators.

The other part of the divine agenda for human beings can be read in the fact that everyone of us is made in the image and likeness of God. Since we are we should be able to live in a freedom that enables both self-determination and participation in the several communities of which we are a part. How explain, then, a U.N. 1993 Human Development report circulating here that claims that 90% of the world's population have no control over the institutions directly affecting their lives? The rural farmer, the economically marginal, immigrants, ethnic and religious minorities are the most powerless to determine their lives according to this report. "Exclusion rather than inclusion is the prevailing reality" of most of the world according to Mahbub ul Haq, the architect of the report.

June 16

This conference evokes very strong and contradictory emotions. In one hour's time you can go from goose pimpled awe at the raw courage of some of the attendees to a stunned disbelief at "man's inhumanity to man." Take torture, for example. In a session I attended this morning I learned that there are seventy seven countries in which torture is performed with the knowledge of or at the instigation of the governments of these countries according to Amnesty International. In one country, Turkey, some 500 of the tortured have been treated in the last two years by the Human Rights Foundation of Turkey. To my great surprise, torture is not ordinarily administered to find out secrets or names but to break the strong personalities of a dissident group.

The tortured one is sent back to the group he has led with the hope that, broken, the will of the group will be broken. The methods of torture are too gruesome to detail; the effects of torture usually last the rest of the victim's life.

The power in this conference is in the indignation of those who have been subjected to indignities and will no longer tolerate this. No matter how dispassionate and staid the upstairs diplomats, the power for placing the world on a new footing is coming from NGOs downstairs. Historically the very notion of rights is a distillation abstracted from indignation. John Shattuck who is the pointman for the US delegation has stressed at our regular briefings that the NGO's and the world wide movement they represent are what the diplomats are responding to.

If governments look at the waves they will miss the tide, for human rights is a tide that is rising unmistakably and inexorably. The Soviet Union and the Eastern Bloc governments kept their eye on the waves and missed the changes in the sea that finally brought them down.

Rights are continually fascinating to me. Every separatist movement I have known has unfurled its banner with their claim.

It seems that without rights the world is in trouble. But with them there is also trouble, in the form of endless division. Would we do better without them? I don't believe so but they are only half the way to justice and peace. The second stage of the journey is the community and its good. If the good of the community doesn't shape the cry for rights then every member of the community becomes his or her own sovereign and whatever communality had been there before is shredded beyond repair.

Self-determination is a destructive force if the one doing the determining does not have the good of the community and its upbuilding at heart. It is a truism that one must couple rights with responsibilities for the comunity and its good. Otherwise rights only heighten individualism and irresponsibility.

June 17

The five Sikhs shrieking their protests outside of this center all morning long has led me to wonder whether the world could become too shrill to be habitable if rights became its lingua franca. Certainly one of the minuses of rights is that they can be so easily manipulated. One of the Indian editors who is living in the same hostel on the other side of town informed me that the protesting Sikhs had lost in a legitimate election and refused to accept their defeat. So this forum afforded them the chance to vent anew hoping to win support for a cause their natural electorate did not buy. (They didn't appear to be winning any new sympathy.) Much more preposterous is the booth set up to win sympathy for Abimael Guzman, the leader of Peru's Shining Path.

That murderer has been apprehended and hopefully will stay behind bars for life. It is a desecration of a holy medium to have such a barbaric cause pose as concerned about human beings and their rights.

Something as sacred as rights have a bad reputation in many places. One of the more subtle ways of exploiting them is to proliferate them so that they become synonymous with or indistinguishable from the interests, of the claimants. Interests whether legitimate or illegitimate, posing as rights make human rights a travesty. The best solution to their exploitation is a greater precision about the contents and foundation of human rights. Our interests are many and few of them, if any, create a moral obligation on others. Our rights are few and, as moral claims, are legitimately made on society because their observance is essential to insuring the human dignity of those making the claim. Multiply these claims and society yawns. The first floor of this Center was a civics workshop for sorting out real rights claims from interested claims that used rights talk to clothe themselves with legitimacy.

June 18

The theme of the conference today was the world's indigenous, aboriginal peoples. Some 50 speakers addressed the upstairs plenary session of delegates, many of them coming from downstairs where the NGO's (non-governmental organizations) are gathered hoping to bring the world's attention to their grievances.

Indigenous people who are estimated by the UN to number some 300 million living in more than 70 countries are descendants of peoples who were living on their lands before settlers came from elsewhere. These new arrivals became dominant through conquest or encroachment and made their own cultures the dominant cultures.

In a number of nations, these indigenous peoples were the first to experience either brutally (by sword or gun) or subtly (by involuntary assimilation) what today we call "ethnic cleansing."

The passionate desire for indigenous peoples to retain their own cultures, languages, lands, and livelihoods is obviously a matter of human rights, political, cultural and economic.

I had a poignant conversation this afternoon with one of the day's speakers, a Kenyan political economist who is also the representative of African indigenous peoples. He himself is a Maasai and in just the story he told me of his once proud tribe's gradual deterioration, the plight of all indigenous peoples can be appreciated. Beginning with the partitioning of Africa by the European nations in 1884, Kimpei Munei's people began to deteriorate. They reside in present day Tanzania and Kenya. Their economy was and is dependent on cattle, sheep and goat herding.

During and after the colonial period they have been forced into smaller land masses and into locales with inadequate water supplies and grazing land as Europeans and wealthier Kenyans and Tanzanians took over their lands. Today these "Lords of East Africa" as they were once called are barely able to feed themselves. Yet their cultural artifacts for which they receive little or no compensation are a thriving industry and the vast territories once held by them are at the heart of the tourism industry which specializes in wild life. Ironically, there is still wild life to see in these game preserves because the Maasai have had a cultural aversion to killing wild animals.

Meanwhile the pressure exerted on indigenous peoples today comes largely from their national governments which are being pressed by the dynamics of an international economy to become more productive by means of modern technologies and better land use methods. You can appreciate the pain of this moment in someone like Dr. Munei who is as sophisticated about modernity as any of us but still very much a member of his people and their culture.

It would take a genius to sort out the rights issues in the case of just this one Maasai tribe.

The issue of the rights of indigenous peoples is a source of enormous tension in our neighbors to the north. At stake is nothing short of the integrity of Canada. The indigenous Cree of Quebec, for example, have already sought for greater self determination and will press all the way for independence if Quebec secedes from the Canadian Federation. To its credit, Canada has already gone further than most countries in meeting the demands of its indigenous groups. Ottawa recently agreed to hand over control of 351,000 square kilometers to its Inuit population. Although the US is not without disputes about the justice done to its indigenous populations, our more acerbic issues are about the civil and cultural rights of minorities and, close on its heels, multiculturalism.

June 19

This is becoming a most memorable experience because there are so many people here who have given their lives to win rights for their people, rights we Americans have grown so accustomed to that we do not even appreciate how rare our experience is or the dangers and depth of the resistance others face daily in seeking their rights.

Wonderful as this is, I find myself often exasperated in conversations here that are in need of a clarification or a distinction that seems to be little understood by many participants, namely, the difference between a positive right and a human right. A positive right is a claim that can be made because there is a law or statute or contract that stipulates the legitimacy of the claim. A positive right has a legal standing.

Thus, I have a right to health benefits, for example, if the contract I have with my employer contains that provision. As long as human rights are confused with positive rights, they suffer from the negatives that are associated with entitlements in our society. Entitlements are legally binding on those who have committed themselves to meet my needs or respond to my claims.

This may be an insurance company, the firm that employs me, the government, etc.

A human right is much less frequent. It may or may not be embodied in a positive right i.e. a law, a statute, a contract, etc. If it is, so much the better. If it is not, that does not mean I do not have a right to make the claim and have it responded to. Human rights are inalienable because they are essential for me to be human and to have a degree of well being commensurate with human dignity. Food, drink, health, shelter are obviously in this category as are the freedoms of association, speech, religion, suffrage. If the Conference sticks to the basic human rights without proliferating them, and adds sanctions to their enforcement, it will be a success. If positive rights are confused with human rights, many here will go home frustrated. Furthermore, a widespread confusion about human rights will continue, leading to rights' inevitable proliferation which in turn will continue to trivialize the very notion of rights and weaken the will of citizens and governments to take them seriously.

June 20

It's beginning to be obvious already that there is going to be a big gap between the final document and the hopes of many who came here. For some, this difference is devastating. I have come to know a Burmese student who presently lives in a kind of limbo outside Bangkok with many other students who have been expelled from Burma since the 1988 uprising. He came here to Vienna full of hope that by bringing attention to the situation of Burma whose legitimately elected government is in exile, that he would win the attention and sympathy needed to get some international leverage and action. Meanwhile his illegitimate government's delegation is upstairs mouthing self serving statements about its care for its citizens.

Although this student wasn't a Christian I spoke to him about my perception of the role rights play in anticipating the final state of the world which Judaism and Christianity calls the reign or kingdom of God. I explained to him that rights were an augur in the present of the relationships we all hope for between ourselves and others, peoples with other peoples and nations with nations. Rights observed are the first fruits of an anticipated perfect harmony. Their violation only creates a thirst for that final harmony. Their observance is evidence in the present that the future will be a flowering of the good we see beginning now.

We live in hope and not in possession of what we hope for, I explained. He seemed buoyed up by this little burst of piety. It is more than a piety, of course. I believe that rights are a secular way of insuring that the sacredness of human life is not thrown to the dogs. He seemed to follow all of this.

I explained what I thought were several immediate values to this symbol of the Kingdom of God. In one way or another it is shared by many of the world's religions so there can be an identification with the vista it opens up. It is, furthermore, a tensive symbol meaning it can take many different forms of expression, narrative or signification. Even more significant for intra-national and international relations, the symbol implies a lag period between the time it takes to understand and act on the ideal and the realization of the ideal. This presumes, therefore, that patience will be built into the pursuit of the rights agenda. There is nothing more deleterious to interpersonal, intergroup and international relations than to generate a high moral earnestness only to be disillusioned. Then anything less than the ideal performance breeds impatience or, worse, intolerance. One of the paradoxes about rights is the amount of hostility they can generate. Ideal performance of the rights agenda awaits the arrival of the new heavens and the new earth.

Meanwhile, the rights agenda functions as a blueprint for a hoped for, ideal future. Present deviations from it and misalignments towards it can be spotted and named for what they are.

June 21

Everyone here seems agreed that women are the most organized and focused on this subject of rights. You can't
move north, east, south or west in these teeming halls
and conference rooms without being impacted by informed women whose data vividly describe the many
modes of violation women are subjected to. Since the
promotion of human rights has been gender blind, they
contend that the redress of gender specific violations
must itself be gender specific. That makes eminent sense
to me. The forms of their violations are rape, sexual har-
rassment, domestic violence, job or wage discrimination
or in the subtler forms of inequality. A Sudanese woman
stunned the plenary today by describing how female cir-
cumcision still violates millions of African women. If their
humiliation and pain were ever to be collectively emitted
she was sure "it would shatter the earth."

My only misgiving about the promotion of women's
rights is what this does to the promotion of human
rights. Is not something lost for the cause itself if half the
human race is concerned about promoting only women's
rights? It would seem to me that it is.

In arguing this I have become aware that every violation of human rights, for example, of a minority, has a
note of a violation of the human dignity of some subset
of humanity. The will and power for promoting human
rights always comes from particular violations and the indignation generated by those violations. But if the only
promotion of rights is for the particular rights of the particular group violated, then will the promotion of human
rights as such ever forge the will of the many for the
transformation of societies and of our world? Although
the generation of indignation is essential to build will
about a given violation, at the same time, the move from

the particular to the universal is essential for the cause of human rights to consolidate into a global movement to insure a universal basis for human dignity.

Those involved with seeking redress for particular violations must come to see the communalities between their grievances and those experienced by others. If they can, a kind of conversion to world citizenship can come about. There are the beginnings of this conversion going on here as the NGO's speak to one another.

Human rights has a way of propelling one into an experience of, a desire for, even a conversion to world citizenship that no other ethical concept I know of can. The coalescence of a world-envisioning citizenry gathered under an indivisible panoply of human rights will insure a moral future for the planet.

June 22

For those who are merely uninvolved bystanders in this cause of promoting human dignity through human rights, it seems to me that a direct knowledge of the global, growing violation of children is more likely to move them beyond indifference to becoming participants in a rights cause than any of the previously mentioned items.

The uninterpreted facts about children: Wars have cost the lives of a half-million children in the last twelve months. In the past decade more than four million children have been maimed by wars.

Twelve million children are presently without the homes they lived in before hostilities. Five million children are presently in refugee camps, most of them with one parent or no parents. Before 1945, the majority of wars' victims were soldiers. In the 150 wars fought since then, 80% of the 20 million who have been killed and 60% of the wounded have been civilians, most of them women and children. In the Sudan alone, thirteen children have died for every soldier lost in combat. Thirty-five thousand children die daily due to malnutrition or disease, both of which are eminently treatable. This list of horrors leaves out an even more damnworthy fact that child prostitution is one of the world's growing industries. According to this week's *Time,* there are an estimated 800,000 underage prostitutes in Thailand, 400,000 in India, 250,000 in Brazil, 60,000 in the Philippines, somewhere between 90,000 and 300,000 in the U.S. The sick thing about this growth in child prostitutes is the assumption by the clients that the younger the prostitute, the less likely he or she is HIV-positive or AIDS stricken. (The opposite is true: the younger the child, the greater the likelihood of lesions and, therefore, susceptibility to infection.)

All of that is the bad news. The good news is that in 1989, the United Nations adopted The Convention on the Rights of the Child. Since that time, 139 countries have ratified it, meaning this Convention becomes the signatory country's guideline for its laws and social programs concerning children. (The U.S. has neither signed nor ratified it.) The goal UNICEF aims at is that by 1995, the UN's 50th anniversary, every country in the world will have ratified it, making it "the first truly global law of humankind."

One of Isaiah's futurist visions foresees a time when "a little child will lead them" (Isaiah 11:6). Since this Child's Rights Convention is being subscribed to with unprecedented rapidity by the nations and is the first treaty in UN history to embody the indivisibility of rights, i.e., it bridges political/civil and social/cultural and economic rights, how right to see a little child leading our world. It is ironic that a Covenant for Children should be on the cutting edge of moral awareness.

Children's plight has moved us to go beyond something that was seen only as a need to be responded to. It has moved up to the moral category of rights on its way to becoming binding international law.

I was impressed with the speech by the head of UNICEF which indicated that this initiative toward children is not merely a matter of hope. Already, in the last decade alone, 20 million children's lives have been saved by a number of programs such as immunization and oral rehydration therapy. Further, a quality of life beyond survival has been made possible for another 100 million children. "Everything we want to achieve for children is a matter of their human rights."

June 23

Liturgically, yesterday was the feast day of two Catholic saints, John Fisher and Thomas More. The quality of a number of people here who, by their lot in life, have been called to be heroic about rights makes me link rights activists with this cloud of witnesses who have gone before us. I hadn't thought of the saints before this as bellweathers to the cause of human rights or models of its advocacy. But so many of them were, as the lives of these two martyrs testify. One of the tasks of future Christi hagiography will be to see the saints as anticipating or promoting the movement of human rights. Clearly there is a secular sanctity in those who today have become singleminded about seeking freedom for whole populations and promoting their dignity in terms of human rights. I hesitate to dub these saints secular since Jesus didn't see them as secular. Recall: "When I was hungry, etc."(Matthew 25:35). But they might be more comfortable being so labeled.

I was thinking about this while talking to one of the refugee's from Tienamen Square this morning. He is one of the founders of a New York-based Center for Human Rights in China. He has the clarity of a Matteo Ricci about what he wants for China. The Gospel he wants all of China to come to hear and to espouse is that of political rights.

June 24

Although I am a member of the national Board of Bread for the World, I had not sufficiently thought through the implications of food as a human right before coming here to Vienna. Several groups here, especially FIAN – whose international headquarters are located in Heidelberg, Germany – see the issue differently than we do in the U.S. Instead of citizens having a right to make a claim on the state or society to provide them with food when they cannot feed themselves, FIAN sees the human right to food as a right to feed oneself. They derive their interpretation from the references to food in the Declaration on Human Rights in 1948, in the Covenant on Social, Cultural and Economic Rights in 1976, and in the guidelines issued by the UN for complying with the latter. Once a government ratifies the ESCR Covenant, it commits itself to seeing that everyone has "adequate food" to observing the "fundamental right of everyone to be free from hunger" (Article 11,1&2). It does this in a way that is not an obligation of the state to feed the hungry but to begin "to take steps . . . to the maximum of available resources . . . for achieving progressively the full realization of the rights" in question, i.e., to food. Secondly, the ratifying state is obliged to make reports to the UN every five years on the particular measures they have taken to insure this right. They are to describe the steps they have taken to improve the food system, its production and distribution. Also the measures relating to "developing or reforming the agrarian systems" (Article 11,2) are to be reported. Since the equitable distribution of food production must be done according to need, the market will not be the sole instrument determining distribution. Hence, the market loses its autonomy.

The UN guidelines imply that a government's responsibility is to maintain the systems that secure access to food rather than to be the actual feeder of its citizens. One of those systems, obviously, is employment. Jobs are the means most people in the world use to feed themselves and their families. The right to food and the right to work are complementary and at the core of the realization of human dignity. States ratifying the ESCR Covenant pledge themselves to make full employment a goal of their policies and social programs.

In their five year reports, ratifying states are to indicate to the UN the measures they have taken towards the achievement of the goals elaborated in the Covenant. ESCR rights become goals to be achieved. Perfection is not expected upon ratification of the Covenant, only commitment to becoming a state that has the Covenant's human rights guiding its values and legislation.

One of the notes played in the Preamble of the ESCR Covenant keeps this thing of rights from becoming an impersonal, bureaucratic, top down, states-only business. It stresses that the individual citizen has "duties to other individuals and to the community to which he/she belongs, [and] is under a responsibility to strive for the promotion and observance of the rights recognized in the present Covenant." If rights are moral obligations on a state they are no less so for individual citizens who in aggregate create the state's obligation to act in terms of rights. Therefore, food is not only everyone's right, it is everyone's responsibility. In our own country, it is clearer to our citizens that it is a responsibility than that it is a right. Soup kitchens and the like have increased from 10,000 in 1980 to 100,000 in 1991. Now, charity is the likely motivation for this impressive outlay of private-sector generosity, for charity readily responds to need. Yet, as good as it is in interpersonal relations, charity is too uncertain a basis on which to create and maintain the programs needed to ensure human dignity. It would be better if that generosity had, as a sort of safety net, a solid foundation of clearly articulated rights. Just as charity responds to need, so justice responds to rights.

In effect, ratifying the Covenant forces a government to spell out, for both its citizens and the international community, how it intends to move from functioning on the unpredictable basis of ad hoc response to need to responding on the basis of moral obligations to embody rights in social programs and policies. Such a Covenant would clarify for citizens both their government's priorities and their personal responsiblities toward ensuring the human dignity of their fellow citizens.

I savor anew Boutros-Ghali's sage advice to make human rights the ultimate norm of our politics. Imagine the difference between a government that didn't have to run on the whim of the electorate and ran with an electorate fully apprized of its own moral responsibilities. How much energy we would have in public life for trying to do the right thing – which is the rights thing – rather than frittering away our moral capital on partisan bickering, popularity polls, interest jockeying, etc. I think we have bungled by not ratifying this Covenant long ago.

Is it too much to hope for that nations could be moved to being competitive with one another morally? We have known international athletic competition, economic competition, military competition, political competition. Could there be a new kind of prize, a Nobel rights prize, awarded to a nation for approaching excellence in bringing their public policies into an alignment with human rights? Or are we too cynical even to imagine such a future?

June 25

The Conference has concluded today. Reactions, beyond the relief shared by all, are mixed. The most negative assessment of the Conference, which I disagree with, is by the head of Amnesty International, Pierre Sane, whose organization has been at the forefront of human rights activism for decades. His criticisms are many, especially the allowance of "national and regional particularities" in the pursuit of human rights since with this concession "the international system of protection has been weakened." Although the final document does fall short of a far-sighted agenda for the 21st century, as many had hoped for, it does advance the cause of human rights on many fronts – notably women, children, and indigenous peoples, the idea of the right to development both individual and collective, plus the General Assembly's awareness that a United Nations High Commissioner for Human Rights should be considered by that body.

The reason I disagree with Sane and others who have complained about this conference is because, from where I sit, it seems naive to think that a more advanced rights platform could have been forged at this time. I have two reasons for my opinion. One of these I implied at the beginning of this diary, the still underanalyzed character of individual rights in the 1948 Declaration and in the subsequent Conventions. Further, in the long view of history, human rights as a principle guiding human relations is still fairly young and is still only gradually being understood. I am aware, for example, how little the world's religious traditions have appropriated them into their teachings. The second reason is that rights are necessarily woven through the maddening complexities of politics, never an easy weave.

When rights are part of a people's narrative, they will have a privileged place in their politics. Political rights are at the heart of our country's story and are easily promoted by us throughout the world for that reason. But social, cultural, and economic rights have as hard a time being appropriated by us as political rights have with other countries' stories. Whether they will be appropriated by us remains to be seen. The point here is the need for patience about rights. The cause of rights is disserved when they are pushed further and faster than is prudent or realistic, given a people's history. For all their merits, virtues, and sometimes heroism, rights activists have to take a longer view of history. Absent such their impatience polarizes those who do not share their vision and can even poison them against the very idea of rights.

One of the ways either or both families of rights make their way into the mindset and values of a nation is via the religious traditions of its citizens. I think, for example, of the virtual silence that greeted the U.S. Catholic Bishops' Conference's Pastoral "Justice for All" when it produced its negative evaluation of the U.S. economy for functioning independently of (economic) human rights. Even in that fine letter, the weave between the story scripturally told and the elaboration of rights that followed was lumpy.

Until the story of Christianity is conveyed to the next generation in terms that have fully-appropriated human rights, the political will of the representatives of the people will do what this group of representatives did, namely "their best," because they took to Vienna a way of thinking and valuing that still sees rights as adventitious to morality. Lone voices have made efforts to link the Gospel, the Commandments, and the Beatitudes to human rights; love of neighbor and enemy has at times been fleshed out in human rights terms. But these voices have been infrequent; they have sung outside the chorus. Until they are brought to the center and lead the whole Christian chorus and the combined religious choruses of the world, it will not be a place where humans know an inalienable dignity, and their sacredness will not be safeguarded by the observance of their rights. This is not only a do-able agenda, it is a must. There is no other transcultural, universal moral concept available to human beings to take the measure of their relationships with one another.